Advance

"Our world is facing uncertainties never seen before. Designing winning strategies, as tough as it can be, is only part of the challenge facing senior management. The most difficult part is to continuously translate our strategy into superior performance at all levels of our organisations. That's what this book is all about: tips and tricks to get things done"
Gérard Mestrallet | CEO | GDF SUEZ

"This book absolutely nails the three things every manager needs to know about strategy – execution, execution, execution!"
Bill Saubert | Regional Business Leader Australia/New Zealand | MasterCard Advisors

"Strategy Execution Heroes is a wonderfully written and well-organised book with a clear commonsense approach to strategy implementation. It is a must-read for any manager regardless of position or years of experience"
Michael Benavente | Managing Director Watches | Gucci

"Organisations have become very aware that much great strategy is lost before it's turned into performance, mainly as a result of poor execution skills. This book is a significant step towards addressing that gap: it takes strategy to the manager level, providing practical everyday recipes to make sure that the 'big picture' does not remain a boardroom abstraction"
Bruno Lanvin | Executive Director, eLab | INSEAD

"Strategy Execution Heroes provides leaders with a practical strategy execution how-to guide which includes a brilliant summary of Jeroen's personal experiences combined with an extensive collection of best practices from leading experts in this field"
Martin Jensen | Head of North America LTE Services | Nokia Siemens Networks

"Strategy Execution Heroes is a refreshingly different approach to strategy implementation. In an extremely pragmatic and actionable way, it puts managers and their individual roles at the centre of the execution pathway rather than the organisation and its systems. Well worth reading!"
Michel Hofland | Finance Director | L'Oreal

"Strategy is a fascinating field, but time and time again we see brilliant strategies fall down due to poor execution. Strategy Execution Heroes really hits the spot by showing what can be done to drive successful execution. I highly recommend this book to strategists and business leaders striving for maximum impact"
Bart Sweerman | Senior Director Internet Business Solutions Group | Cisco

"Even the best strategy is worthless if you are unable to get it implemented. Execution is key and Strategy Execution Heroes explains how to do it"
Matthieu Crépey | Former Retail Director | L'Occitane

"This book takes a refreshingly different approach to Strategy Execution. Most importantly, it is hands-on and presents new perspectives on known problems. Inspiring input for practitioners!"
Prof. Dr Frederik Ahlemann | European Business School Germany

"Strategy Execution Heroes takes a different approach to all other books that I have read on Strategy Execution. Most importantly, it focuses on the manager and his individual role in the implementation of strategy rather than on the organisation. A breath of fresh air!"
Thilo Kusch | CFO and Board member | Magyar Telecom

"This book is a compelling read that drives right to the heart of successful and flawless strategy execution. Many other strategy books float in the clouds of organizational theory, but this is what we really need – practical, specific and hard-hitting direction and real-life advice"
Jeffrey Stephen Kehoe | Regional Head Bancassurance Asia | AXA

"Practical, structured and with proven advice; exactly what a manager needs"
Karel Van Eetvelt | Managing Director | UNIZO

"Strategy Execution Heroes helps you build the foundation to champion and communicate strategy within your company. And it contains great insights from well known executives that I found immediately helpful for my organisation"
Phillip Shoemaker | Director Applications Technology | Apple

"Strategy Execution Heroes gives a pragmatic series of hands-on tips and tricks to help implement your ideas. Not all of them fit my situation. However, those which do are absolute breakthroughs!"
Armin Knapp | Senior Controller | Salzgitter AG

STRATEGY EXECUTION HEROES

BUSINESS STRATEGY IMPLEMENTATION AND STRATEGIC MANAGEMENT DEMYSTIFIED

A PRACTICAL PERFORMANCE MANAGEMENT GUIDEBOOK FOR THE SUCCESSFUL LEADER

Jeroen De Flander

the performance factory | *it's all about strategy execution*

- Strategy Execution Heroes: expanded edition -

Business strategy implementation and strategic management demystified: a practical performance management guidebook for the successful leader

Published by *the performance factory*
Louizalaan 149/24 Avenue Louise, 1050 Brussels, Belgium
www.the-performance-factory.com
Cover design: Uncompressed

To report errors, please send a note to errata@the-performance-factory.com

Publications of *the performance factory* are available via amazon.com or amazon.co.uk. For bulk purchases, please contact bulk@the-performance-factory.com

ISBN 978-908148734-4
D/2010/12.173/1
NUR: 801, 808 | BIC: KJC, KJMB | BISAC: BUS063000, BUS071000, BUS059000
Keywords: Strategy, Leadership, Skills

Dedicated to
Karen, Lauren and Jonas,
my heroes

JOIN THE CRUSADE AGAINST STRATEGY TOURISTS

You are reading the expanded edition of Strategy Execution Heroes. Additions to the January 2010 first edition are two completely new chapters, 12 new downloads and a free 60-minute audio recording from the Next Generation Strategy event during which I shared the stage with Michael Porter.

The last two years have been very exciting. For the first time since the nineties of advocating the importance of Strategy Execution when I worked for strategy consultancy Arthur D. Little, I feel that the balance has shifted. Strategy Execution is recognised within organisations and universities as crucial to business success, as well as in the wider world. By the end of this year, I will have talked about my passion in more than 30 countries on five continents, including well-established markets such as the US or the UK and fast-growing economical players like China and Brazil, big countries like Russia and smaller ones, such as Iceland.

But the crusade isn't yet over!

Take a moment to think about your own organisation and the people working there. I'm sure you will agree there are still many strategy tourists – those managers who lack the motivation, skills and knowledge to turn a strategy into performance – running around.

So I hope you will join me in the crusade against these strategy tourists. I hope you will become an execution ambassador and promote the importance of Strategy Execution at every opportunity.

Want to get in touch? Drop me an email at jeroen@jeroen-de-flander.com or connect using LinkedIn.

Kind regards

Jeroen De Flander

Strategy Execution ambassador
March 2012

ABOUT THE AUTHOR

Jeroen De Flander is a seasoned international Strategy Execution expert, top executive coach, seminar leader and highly regarded keynote speaker.

Jeroen has helped more than 19,500 managers in 24 countries master the necessary execution skills.

He is co-founder of *the performance factory* – a leading research, training and advisory firm which is solely focused on helping individuals and organisations increase performance through best-in-class Strategy Execution.

For several years, he was the responsible manager worldwide of the Balanced Scorecard product line for Arthur D. Little – a leading strategy consulting firm.

The 50+ companies he has advised on various strategy execution topics include Atos Worldline, AXA, Base, Bridgestone, CEMEX, the Flemish and Belgian governments, GDFSuez, Honda, ING, Johnson & Johnson, Komatsu and Sony.

To book Jeroen to speak at your next event or to run a strategy execution seminar for your company, please contact him through his website www.jeroen-de-flander.com.

ABOUT THE EXPERTS

Strategy Execution is a vast domain that required choices to be made about topics covered. It also meant that one person alone could not have the expertise to cover all the topics. The following five experts have therefore contributed to this book.

Each of them helped me in the writing process by delivering content and challenging ideas. A summary of their experience and credentials follows.

Dr. Peter Scott-Morgan is acknowledged as the foremost authority on communication and change behaviour. Combining complementary expertise in management science, sociology and information technology, he is the best-selling author of six non-fiction books. He has taught MBA courses at the London Business School, the Rotterdam School of Management and the ADL School of Management at Boston College. He is in constant demand as a speaker, consultant and teacher and has given over 1000 speeches, presentations and workshops around the world. His book *Unwritten Rules of the Game* was voted one of the top 25 business books in the year of its release.

Sir John Whitmore is regarded as the world's best coach and founder of performance coaching. He has written five books on sport, leadership and coaching, of which *Coaching for Performance* is the best known having sold 500,000 copies in 17 languages. Honoured with the President's Award by the International Coach Federation (ICF), rated the number one business coach by *The Independent* newspaper and as having had the most impact on the coaching profession by the UK Association of Coaching, John is one of the leading figures in the international coaching community. He is a pre-eminent thinker in leadership and organisational change and works globally with leading multinational corporations to establish coaching management cultures and leadership programmes.

Volker Voigt is an acknowledged initiative management expert. He is a well-known speaker on project events and co-author of a number of books on the subject. For several years, Volker was Arthur D. Little's responsible manager for developing and applying project management methodologies in large and complex client projects. In 2000, he founded Cataligent, a leading provider of web-based enterprise project systems which today has 5,000+ users worldwide. Some of the companies that use the software are Lufthansa, Adidas, Vattenfall, Thomas Cook, Bertelsmann, US Postal Services, AGCO and Korea Thrunet.

Vincent Lion is an expert in strategy, innovation and technology management with a focus on the related competences' development. He teaches MBA courses at Solvay Business School, United Business Institutes and the University of Novi Sad in Serbia. As a management consultant, he helps leading companies like KBC, GDFSuez and Belgacom design and implement ambitious strategies and build the supporting competence centres. His workshops on developing strategic, innovative and technological competences are widely recognised as achieving exceptional business results.

Koen Schreurs is a Strategy Execution expert who specialises in aligning individual performance to the business strategy. As former Managing Director of GITP Belgium – a leading HR consultancy – he has an in-depth knowledge of individual performance management. His background as management consultant within the Arthur D. Little Strategy & Organisation division has provided him with the expertise and experience to forge the links between individual and organisational performance. He is co-founder of *the performance factory* where he heads up all surveys and benchmarking projects and related R&D efforts. His professional clients include Allianz, AstraZeneca, Bayer, Bridgestone, Brussels Airport, DeltaLloyd, GDFSuez, ING and the Belgian Government.

Carlos Guevara is a seasoned consultant and trainer who specialises in Strategy Execution. He has led various projects in the public and private sectors in numerous industries throughout the Americas, Europe and the Middle East. A partner at ShiftIN Partners, an UAE based consulting firm, Carlos co-authored Designing a Sound Governance System to Drive Strategic Transformation at ADWEA which was published in the September-October 2011 issue of the Balanced Scorecard Report (available from the Harvard Business Publishing website www.hbr.org). He is also the author of Executing Strategy in the Midst of the 'Perfect Storm'.

CONTENTS AT A GLANCE

CONTENTS

PART 1   GET TO KNOW THE 8

PART **2** ACT WITHIN THE 8

PART 4 FEED THE 8

Superman on a 'Strategy Rescue' mission

Superman, otherwise known as Clark Kent, flies into the office. Instead of his usual red cape, he has decided to wear his three-piece grey pinstriped Armani suit. *"It just seems more appropriate"* he had thought while getting ready that morning.

Superman is reacting to a 'failing strategy' distress call from 53-year-old Mike, CEO of Magnatexx, a large pharmaceutical company. It was the 267th call he had received in the two weeks since starting his new sideline – the 'strategy rescue' programme.

When he arrives at Magnatexx, Superman immediately identifies the execution issues and takes over the role of all managers. In no time at all, Magnatexx obtains the desired competitive advantage and performance starts to peak. And everyone lives happily ever after.

This story seems too good to be true. And it is.

But you don't have to be able to fly like Superman, scale walls like Batman or become green and super strong like the Incredible Hulk to turn a great strategy into great performance.

You need performance-driven managers who master Strategy Execution.

Strategy Execution is no longer 'the gap nobody knows', the title of the first chapter of the best-seller *Execution*. Thanks to the authors Bossidy and Charan, Strategy Execution pioneers Kaplan and Norton, several leading articles in respected business magazines such as *The Harvard Business Review* and a host of research, organisations have become very aware that much great strategy is lost before it's turned into performance mainly as a result of poor execution skills.

The performance gap is known. And it's time for companies to close it.

This book will help you get the job done. *Strategy Execution Heroes* will help you to:

1. Approach Strategy Execution from a manager's perspective.
2. Align individual and organisational performance in a simple, easy-to-communicate, sexy Strategy Execution framework.
3. Communicate your strategy effectively.
4. Set great objectives for yourself and your team members.
5. Coach others through the implementation maze.
6. Simplify your Strategy Execution process.
7. Select, manage and deliver your strategic initiatives.
8. Set up a development platform to boost the execution skills of others in the organisation.
9. Turn Strategy Execution into a competitive advantage.

In short, this book will help you get the execution job done. But don't expect complex theories or fancy words. *Strategy Execution Heroes* gets right to the point and won't waste your time. It will:

- *Boost your learning* with 300+ practical tips revealed by senior executives from BT, Coca-Cola, Lockheed Martin, eBay and many others.

- *Inspire your thinking* with useful insights from top experts such as Sir John Whitmore, Dr Peter Scott-Morgan and Prof Vincent Lion.

- *Put your action plan on the right track* with 39 valuable downloads.

So whether you are a future manager preparing for the challenge, a manager in the field or an experienced senior executive, get ready to boost your execution skills. Become a Strategy Execution hero and turn your great strategy into great performance.

INTRODUCTION

Start your journey

Dear Reader,

You are about to start discovering *Strategy Execution Heroes*. To help you get the most out of this experience, I have added some comments and suggestions.

1. ***Download supporting material.*** This book contains more than 300 tips, which you will find on almost every page. And you can download even more supporting material including self-assessments, examples, extra tips, reading lists and workshop guidelines.

   For your convenience, I've added an overview of all 39 available downloads on page 9. The downloads themselves can be found at www.strategy-execution-heroes.com/downloads. Your access code is the fourth word on page 126.

Where you see a box such as this one with a ⬇ in front, supporting material is available at the website www.strategy-execution-heroes.com/downloads

---

2. ***Be inspired by stories from the field.*** Eight senior executives from different fields and industries share their visions of Strategy Execution.

At the end of each of the chapters in Parts 2 and 3, one of them gives you tried and tested insights to inspire your actions.

There's a short overview of all the senior executives involved on page 8, along with the page references.

3. *Follow your 'learning' logic.* The first two chapters provide a general overview. You don't necessarily need to read them *per se* to understand the others – although, of course, they will help if you're fairly new to Strategy Execution. So feel free to start reading from the beginning, or alternatively with the chapter that intrigues you the most. It's up to you.

4. *Remember the 80/20 rule.* This book is loaded with ideas and suggestions. But not all of them will have the same impact when executed.

Be selective. Pick your battles. And direct 80 percent of your energy to those 20 percent of the ideas that you think will boost progress. Most of the key sections have self-assessment downloads to help you direct your focus.

5. *Study alone, with a coach or a whole group.* Embark on a self-study course, involve your coach or discuss your findings with colleagues. I have indicated where team discussions would be appropriate. For some of them, workshop templates are available for download.

6. *Embark on a learning journey.* I'm delighted that you are ready to get reading because it means you are interested in Strategy Execution, my passion. I'm certain that the book will help you after the first read, but in order to maximise your learning experience, you should read it more than once. Embark on a learning journey and keep your copy close to hand as your Strategy Execution travel guide.

7. *Keep up-to-date and exchange ideas.* Strategy Execution is a vast area in constant evolution. Stay up-to-date with the latest developments, collect more tips or exchange ideas with fellow Strategy Execution devotees. There are a number of ways to keep yourself on top of the game:

- *Join Linked SE (Strategy Execution group),* the official Strategy Execution group on LinkedIn, the premier professional network on the internet. Go to www.linkedin.com/groupRegistration?gid=2325487.
- *Subscribe to* the performance factory newsletter. Go to www.the-performance-factory.com/register.
- *Write to me.* I would be very interested in your Strategy Execution tips and suggestions. You can drop me an email at jeroen@jeroen-de-flander.com or use the contact page on my website www.jeroen-de-flander.com/contact.

Jeroen De Flander
www.jeroen-de-flander.com

Senior executives sharing their views of Strategy Execution – an overview

Overview of the 39 available downloads

1. *The Strategy Execution Barometer®: research report* – a summary.
2. Link your objectives with the next level up – a template.
3. Interesting leadership resources.
4. How to give effective feedback – tips.
5. *The Pyramid Principle* – training module.
6. A great communication model – training module.
7. Great books on writing – a list.
8. Improve your podium performance – tips.
9. Evaluate the quality of your strategy communication – a checklist.
10. Build a professional strategy communication plan – 'how to' guide.
11. High-quality coaching questions – examples.
12. Select the right coaching tips – a checklist.
13. Score your Strategy Execution process – self-assessment.
14. Boost your Strategy Execution process – guideline overview.
15. Boost your Strategy Execution process – workshop format.
16. Write a great performance story – an example.
17. Write a great performance story – workshop format.
18. Best-in-class initiative management – a checklist.
19. Best-in-class initiative management – workshop format.
20. Interesting project management resources.
21. How to set up a strategy office – tips.
22. Score your management development mistakes – self-assessment.
23. Create a solid development platform – a checklist.
24. Create a solid development platform – workshop format.
25. Define your future capabilities – workshop format.
26. High-quality competency dictionary – an example.
27. A Strategy Execution master class – agenda.
28. Introduce a Balanced Scorecard approach – a checklist.
29. Introduce a Balanced Scorecard approach – workshop format.
30. Advanced Balanced Scorecard tips – a checklist.
31. Advanced Balanced Scorecard tips – workshop format.
32. Measuring frameworks – examples.
33. Great books on strategy – a reading list.
34. The Next Generation Strategy Event – my slide set.
35. The Next Generation Strategy Event – 60 minute audio MP3.
36. 3 generations CSR: Donators, Avoiders and Creators – my slide set.
37. Spice up your strategy process – a checklist.
38. Spice up your strategy process – workshop format.
39. Typical steps in an industry analysis – overview

Downloads available at www.strategy-execution-heroes.com/downloads

PART 1

GET TO KNOW THE 8

CHAPTER I

A new mathematical enigma: performance 0+0=8

"However beautiful the strategy,
you should occasionally look at the results"
– Sir Winston Churchill

"Don't measure your performance by what you have
accomplished, but by what you should have
accomplished within your capabilities"

"Strategy Execution is all about realising the full
potential of your strategy – and not limiting yourself
to only 50, 60 or 70 percent"

I magine you run a removals company. And every day, of the 100 box-es you move for your customers, you lose 60 of them. How long do you think you would stay in business?

Or imagine you are a tennis player. And every match you play, you hit every other ball into the net. How many matches do you think you would win?

According to research published in *The Harvard Business Review*, *"Companies realise only 40-to-60 percent of their strategies' potential value*". The rest is lost on the way or never makes it over the net.

The numbers don't look great – and over the last 10 years many companies have started to realise that it takes much more than a great strategy to be number one in their industry. You need to turn that great strategy into great performance.

That's where Strategy Execution comes in. It bridges the gap between brilliant strategies and superior performance. Led by Balanced Scorecard inventors Kaplan and Norton and best-selling authors Bossidy and Charan, Strategy Execution has become a fast-growing bleep on the radar screens of top executives.

But simply appearing on that radar is not enough to make it happen. Each company, large or small, needs to master crucial Strategy Execution skills.

In Chapter 1 we look at where companies lose performance and zoom in on how sound Strategy Execution can help.

How much potential performance are you losing?

So Strategy Execution is no longer the black hole that drains performance. Organisations today are aware of the performance lost through bad Strategy Execution.

But in order to take the next step – to close that gap – organisations need a more detailed view on *exactly* where they are losing performance.

Knowing that your organisation loses between 40 and 60 percent of its strategic potential on the execution highway between the city 'strategy' and the city 'performance', is an interesting fact but doesn't really help solve your problem.

Twelve years ago, I started collecting detailed Strategy Execution data as I was fascinated by the implementation black box that was costing organisations millions.

Today, the database managed by *the performance factory*, is probably one of the largest Strategy Execution databases in the world, with data from more than 1100 companies, 29 industries and 36 countries.

On the site www.the-performance-factory.com you can download a free summary or buy the Strategy Execution Barometer®, a detailed bench-mark report that will compare your implementation strengths and weak-nesses with your industry peers and the overall market.

Here are some interesting facts. Of all respondents:

- 15 percent believes that the strategy is the wrong one for their company.
- About one-in-three – 30 percent – receives no information on how to execute the strategy.
- Only 61 percent is convinced that the strategic initiatives are staffed with the right people.
- As few as 27 percent believes that the strategic initiatives are being managed correctly.
- 27 percent doesn't receive any individual feedback.
- 17 percent indicates that performance isn't monitored.
- 38 percent indicates that poor performers don't face any con-sequences.
- 18 percent is unable to explain how to translate the strategy or set individual objectives.
- 27 percent receives no training on essential management skills.
- Only 57 percent do not question the objectivity of appraisals.

In short: the results indicate that initiative management is the weak-est link in the execution chain, followed by strategy communication and skills development. The complexity of the Strategy Execution process comes in fourth place.

 Performance download 1. *The Strategy Execution Barometer®: research report* – a summary.

What's in a name? Strategy Execution defined

Strategy Execution can be defined as 'all the actions necessary to turn your strategy into success'. But this short definition won't help you very much in getting a better grasp of the discipline.

So let's go beyond this single-line explanation and take a broader look at Strategy Execution. Here are 12 insights:

1. ***Strategy Execution is a vast area with blurred borders.*** It includes several processes – from budgeting to evaluating individual objectives, and involves all functional domains.

2. ***Strategy Execution is a discipline of its own.*** Making strategy work isn't the same as strategy making. It's a different game with its own rules, potential pitfalls and best practices. Four important differentiators are:

   - *It involves everyone.* From the CEO to the blue-collar worker, everyone is involved in executing the strategy. Their roles might be different, but all individuals contribute to the organisation's execution effort.
   - *It takes much longer.* You can build a strategy in a few weeks (or months at the most) but the execution can take several years. It's a sprint versus a marathon.
   - *It demands short- and long-term thinking.* While executing, you need to manage your long-term implementation plan *and* worry about the nitty-gritty actions you will take tomorrow.
   - *It requires a specific skill set.* A different game demands different skills. The most important strategy skill by far is analytical thinking, whereas executioners particularly benefit from strong objective setting and people skills such as communication and coaching.

> *"Execution is a specific set of behaviours and techniques that companies need to master in order to have competitive advantage. It's a discipline of its own"*
> – Ram Charan and Larry Bossidy, *Execution*

3. ***Great Strategy Execution requires a great strategy.*** Even if Strategy Execution differs greatly from strategy building, it cannot

exist without it. In fact, a great execution can never compensate for a poor strategy.

4. ***Strategy Execution requires your attention from the start.*** And the start is the strategy formulation phase. Execution isn't something you worry about after you have already finished crafting your strategy.

You need to think about the implementation challenges *at the same time* you design your strategy.

Here's an overview of the five most important implementation hazards to think about while developing your strategy. To give you a head start, I have included for each one, the key question(s) to ask during the strategy design phase:

- *The existing culture*. Strategies that demand a large cultural shift are doomed to failure as cultural change is very hard to accomplish. Ask yourself: 'How big is the culture change needed in order to execute the new strategy?' and 'Is the required change realistic?'.
- *The existing power structures*. Each organisation has its own power structures, invisible at the surface and part of the 'unwritten rules' within the organisation. But they *do* exist. And they *will* influence your execution capabilities. Pose the following questions: 'What are the current power structures in our organisation?' and 'How will they impact the implementation of the strategy we are developing?'.
- *The ability to change*. Each strategy will demand a change effort. And I can tell you the effort is always bigger than you anticipate at the start. Ask yourself: 'How much change can our organisation handle?'.
- *The maturity of the execution process*. Once finished, the strategy will use the existing execution processes in your organisation. Upgrading is possible but takes time. So ask yourself: 'What's the current maturity of our execution capabilities?', 'Is there a need to upgrade?' and 'How long will the upgrade realistically take to accomplish?'.
- *The maturity of the Strategy Execution skills*. Related to previous. Processes need skilled people to operate them. The questions

to ask: 'What's the current maturity of the manager's execution skills?', 'Is there a need to upgrade?' and 'How long will the upgrade realistically take to accomplish?'.

> *"Culture eats strategy for lunch, every day"*
> – Dick Clark, CEO, Merck

5. ***Strategy Execution has a strong timing sequence.*** You don't do everything at the same time. One thing happens before the other, and the order is important.

6. ***Strategy Execution requests a seamless integration between organisational and individual performance.*** You can look at performance from either an organisational or an individual perspective. But in order to realise your strategy, a connection between both is crucial. Most will agree with this statement, but few will actually make it happen.

> *"Building a visionary company requires one percent vision and 99 percent alignment"*
> – Jim Collins and Jerry Porras, *Built to Last*

7. ***Strategy Execution demands clear responsibilities.*** Strategy Execution takes place across different organisational levels. Depending on the size of the company, these include the overall company level, one or more intermediate levels – usually called division, department or team – and the individual level.

In large organisations, you can have up to 10 different parties involved, including corporate functions, functional lines, regional structures and countries. In addition, within each of these structures, responsibilities are often dispersed among the departments of human resources, finance and strategy and the various leadership teams.

Pretty easy to lose some of your strategy in this structure, wouldn't you say?

So in order to make it work, you need to define clear responsibilities for all parties involved.

8. **Strategy Execution requires horizontal alignment**. Building on the previous point, I'd like to stress the importance of a strong horizontal collaboration between business and support departments. Their relationship should go beyond the annual budget and monthly operational meetings.

9. **Strategy Execution needs heroes.** Managers are the most important players in the execution contest. In fact, strategy remains a paper exercise without managers taking the right actions and fulfilling their roles. They contribute content, are the links between organisational levels, and act as performance role models.

And this requires the right attitude. Execution isn't something *others* should worry about. Each manager should:
   - Acknowledge the importance of Strategy Execution.
   - Understand what Strategy Execution is all about.
   - See execution as an essential part of being a leader.
   - Know how to maximise their crucial role in the whole process.
   - Develop the necessary Strategy Execution skills.

On top of that, senior managers need to put the necessary processes in place to ensure that all managers in the organisation become execution heroes. This is a challenge in itself.

> *"Strategy Execution isn't something other people should worry about while you are doing something far more important"*

10. **Strategy Execution asks for measurement.** In many organisations, Strategy Execution is still a black box. You throw your strategy in one end and performance comes out the other end. But nobody really knows what did the trick. It's impossible to say what worked

and what didn't. Even worse, companies change things for the worse because they don't know the key elements of their execution success.

So, as with all other business activities, organisations need to measure their performance. It's time to open the implementation box and see what's inside. Here's how:

- *Find the strong and weak points of your execution process.* If possible, compare them against your competitors. Evaluate the complete process or zoom in on one or two steps. Do the exercise for the organisation, one or more divisions, or start with only a small team.
- Once you have gained these insights, *focus your energy on those things that matter most* for the organisation. In other words, set priorities.
- *Don't forget to keep doing what you do well.* Once you've identified your strong points, make sure you keep them best-in-class.
- *Have a long-term perspective.* It takes time to build capabilities. Small organisations should count on 18 months to become best-in-class. For a large multinational, it can take up to three years to get there. Your measurement approach should take the long-term into account.
- *Set intermediate goals and measure your progress.* While you do want a long-term measurement perspective, you also want to define and track intermediate targets.

11. **Strategy Execution is a resident.** Constantly changing environments, customers, competitors and employees require Strategy Execution to be an ongoing process. It should be institutionalised within the organisation: a permanent activity – part of the organisation's culture and DNA – that is driven with persistence and discipline.

"After a business implements a strategy, competitors will react, and the firm's strategy will need to adapt to meet the new challenges. There is no stopping point and no final battle. The competitive cycle continues on perpetually. Produce and compete or perish"
– Thomas Timings Holme

---

12. ***Strategy Execution is on its way to maturity.*** Robert Kaplan and David Norton started a new management revolution in 1992 with the introduction of their Balanced Scorecard concept.

Originally launched as a new way of measuring strategy, taking into account other measures rather than merely the financial ones, the Balanced Scorecard quickly became the instrument that made managers think harder about the implementation of their strategy.

And today, more than a decade later, Strategy Execution has grown out of its infancy and is on its way to maturity.

The 8 – a unique Strategy Execution framework

Strategy Execution or performance management is a complex process. In fact, it's a mix of several processes – and the ideal process picture is different for each organisation.

But even with a different mix, each best-in-class performance management process should include some basic building blocks. Luckily, many of them are readily available within most organisations. They include:
   – Tried and tested approaches for reviewing a strategy.
   – Strategy cascade tools, the Balanced Scorecard being the best-known.
   – Techniques to structure, execute and monitor strategic projects.
   – A proven approach to set, monitor and evaluate individual objectives.
What is lacking however, is a simple framework to integrate and align all of these different building blocks.

And that's where the 8 comes in. It combines the most important building blocks into a coherent image.

The 8 doesn't cover all of the ins and outs of the Strategy Execution process. It's not supposed to. It's not a rigid step-by-step instruction. But it does provide a necessary, simple framework for Strategy Execution.

You can make your execution framework more complex if you prefer. For the organisational cycle in particular, there are some sophisticated models around. Kaplan and Norton describe one in their latest book *The Execution Premium*. You can find a second one that also includes organisational structure impacts in *Making Strategy Work* by Hrebiniak.

While I like the insights that these conceptual models provide, their complexity makes them unsuitable as a day-to-day Strategy Execution framework for the whole organisation. I believe a Strategy Execution framework for all managers and staff needs to be simple, highly recognisable and sexy. (Think like a marketer and make it stick.)

I'm aware that you will lose some of the nuances, but that's a choice you need to make. Besides, it doesn't mean you have to over-simplify your Strategy Execution process. You can use the 8 for communication purposes and keep a more detailed version to be known only by those who have to organise the process.

Not convinced yet?

Here are two 'content' arguments:

1. The 8 shows the importance of aligning individual and organisational performance, one of the most important things you can do to improve your success rate.
2. The 8 gives initiative management the attention it deserves (read 'needs'). International research from *the performance factory* shows that initiative management is the single most important execution problem that companies face. In other words, it's the place where most performance is lost.

So, if you look for a simple, highly recognisable Strategy Execution framework that emphasises the link between individual and organisational performance and gives initiative management the importance it deserves, go for the 8.

Figure 1. The 8, a unique Strategy Execution framework

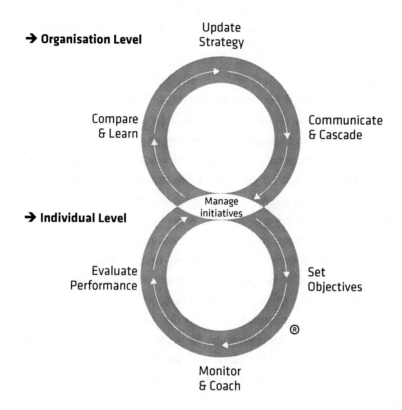

The 8 – crucial building blocks

Here is an overview of the different building blocks:

1. Review and update your strategy

Your strategy is the long-term action plan designed to achieve your vision. Depending on the industry you are in, it maps the road your company should take for the next 3-to-10 years. It's designed to help you gain the competitive advantage over your industry peers.

On a regular basis, usually annually, a company needs (and wants) to update its strategy based on changes in its competitive environment and on the Strategy Execution feedback from the previous cycle.

The execution framework includes strategy updates as they take place on a regular, recurring basis at all levels of the organisation. It excludes the real strategy work, conducted only once every three-to-five years at the top of an organisation.

2. Communicate

As soon as your strategy (or strategy update) is finalised and approved by all stakeholders, you should focus on strategy communication. Transparent and easy-to-understand communication creates the necessary understanding and engagement for the new, adapted strategy.

It is essential to use all available communication platforms. One big strategy event and a single strategy email are not nearly enough. Use other meeting platforms, discussion groups, informal and formal encounters, performance management sessions, intranets, websites, screensavers, coffee rooms, noticeboards etc. to communicate the strategy. *You cannot over-communicate your vision and strategy!*

Pay attention to the quality of your strategy communication. Senior managers as strategy ambassadors, in particular, should be especially careful about how they communicate. In addition to the content itself, tone of voice and presentation skills are essential elements in transferring content and creating the necessary enthusiasm for others to pass on the message. Make sure you don't kill your strategy with poor-quality, uninspiring communication.

3. Cascade

When you cascade your company's strategy, you break down the objectives into smaller chunks for the next organisational level. The process stops at the smallest unit level – often teams. In the end, the size of your organisation will define the size of the cascade.

It is crucial to achieve *macro alignment* between all the objectives – horizontally and vertically – in your organisation. You can achieve better alignment by aiming for MECE – Mutually Exclusive and Collectively Exhaustive. This simply means that everything from the level below (strategy, initiatives, objectives, etc.) should add up exactly to the level above, without any overlaps. This may sound logical and easy, but practice shows that many companies have a difficult time linking levels correctly.

 Performance tip. One of the reasons companies find it hard to get the macro alignment right is the complex matrix of responsibilities. Strategy Execution accountabilities are often blurred and spread across an organisation.

In large organisations, you can have up to 10 different parties involved, including corporate functions, functional lines, regional structures and countries. In addition, within each of these structures, responsibilities are often dispersed among human resources, finance, the strategy department and the various leadership teams.

When your macro alignment doesn't seem to be working, start by taking a look at the complexity of the Strategy Execution accountabilities and reduce where possible.

On a *micro level*, you need to balance your objectives across perspectives. The four traditional perspectives are: financial, customer, internal processes and people. But you can always add other dimensions as appropriate. The Balanced Scorecard is the best-known method.

In addition to the balancing act on the macro and micro levels, you need to select the right indicators – often called Key Performance Indicators or KPIs – to track the objectives and define appropriate targets.

4. Compare and learn

Your strategy is a hypothesis. It's your best estimate of the route to success… but it's still an estimation.

It's crucial to take some time at the end of a cycle to go back and check your hypothesis, to compare your initial strategic assumptions with what you have learnt from the reality of the Strategy Execution cycle that is being completed. By doing this, you will put yourself in the forefront – research shows that only 15 percent of companies take this step.

But at the same time, make sure that you don't just look at your strategy: study your Strategy Execution capability as well. All too often, we see companies jumping automatically to change their strategy because they did not reach their projected performance. But, upon examination, there is nothing wrong with their strategy. The problem is the execution. So don't forget to challenge your implementation capabilities as well!

This 'compare and learn' step will help you verify your hypothesis (read 'review your strategy'), update your strategy, and fine-tune your execution efforts and capabilities accordingly.

5. Manage initiatives

Initiative management is the activity in which your dreams run up against reality, where your strategy meets operations and where resources are added to the strategy formula. It's one of the most difficult Strategy Execution steps and therefore the point where implementation often goes wrong.

Initiative management is all about selecting, prioritising and executing the right strategic initiatives: those actions that will lead to the realisation of your strategy.

6. Set objectives

Setting individual objectives is one of the best things you can do to improve performance – yours, your team's or even that of an entire organisation.

The positive impact of goal setting is one of the most widely researched and scientifically validated aspects of today's organisational science. Two key researchers of goal setting and task motivation theory are Edwin Locke from the University of Maryland and Gary Latham from Toronto University.

Link all individual objectives with the overall strategy. If you don't, you might end up with great individual objectives ... but of no use to the organisation!

Also, focus on the way you secure agreement on the objectives. It's the quality of the objectives – including the link with the overall company strategy – *and* the acceptance of these objectives that will make your individual objective setting a success.

7. Monitor and coach

Regular coaching motivates people and dramatically increases their chances of success. It also simplifies the final performance evaluation. In fact, regular coaching is far more important than the formal review meeting somewhere around the middle of the year.

Providing feedback in the right way – a key coaching skill – is a crucial step in boosting performance.

Performance coaching is a relatively new, but rapidly growing, knowledge field. The leading authority is Sir John Whitmore, author of *Coaching for Performance* and sparring partner for Chapter 5 on coaching.

8. Evaluate performance

Most organisations conduct a formal performance evaluation at the end of the individual performance management cycle. Ideally, the evaluation should answer the question: 'Are the individual performance objectives achieved?'. Be sure you make an honest assessment. Several techniques can help you.

Although it's important to link performance to remuneration, performance evaluation should be a separate process.

The extended 8

Large organisations need several steps to cascade the overall strategy to the individual level. The cascade runs down through business units, functional lines, departments and teams.

For communication purposes, it helps to change the visual. Here's an example:

Figure 2. The extended 8, an example

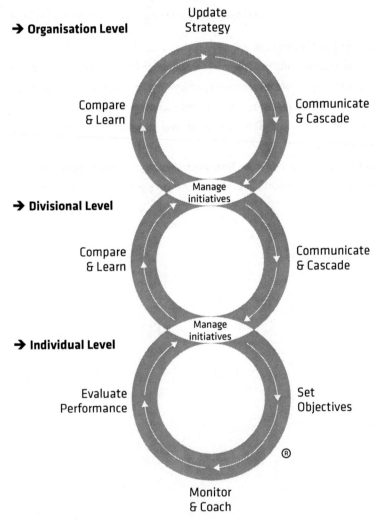

Strategy Execution: your next competitive advantage?

In his best-seller, Jim Collins concludes that strategy doesn't separate the good from the great, execution does. Research from Kaplan and Norton indicates that companies with a formal Strategy Execution system have a two-to-three times better chance of success as those who don't have such a system.

Strategy Execution is a new, emerging competitive battlefield that starts to get more and more attention.

Are you a player in the execution game? Or merely sitting on the sidelines?

Don't limit yourself to your strategy alone to set yourself apart in your industry. Bring your Strategy Execution capabilities into play and turn them into your next competitive advantage.

PERFORMANCE TAKEAWAYS

- Sound Strategy Execution bridges the gap between a great strategy and great performance.
- Strategy Execution is a vast area with blurred borders; a discipline of its own, with its proper skill set.
- In comparison to strategy making, it involves everyone, takes much longer and requires a short- and long-term focus.
- Strategy Execution requires a great strategy to start from and lots of management attention during the strategy formulation phase. A company's culture, power structure, ability to cope with change, quality of the execution process and skills managers, all influence the ability to execute any chosen strategy.
- A Strategy Execution framework orients managers to take the right actions at the right time.
- The 8 is a simple, visually strong and easy-to-communicate Strategy Execution framework that combines individual and organisational performance.
- Thanks to pioneers like Kaplan and Norton and Charan and Bossidy, Strategy Execution isn't the black hole it used to be. Today, most organisations are aware that poor Strategy Execution creates a performance gap.
- So the key question is not *if* there is a gap but *how* it will be closed.
- Unfortunately, due to the complexity of this challenge, companies continue to lose 40-to-60 percent of their strategic potential during the execution phase.
- Organisations need to start by understanding in more detail where the Strategy Execution process leaks performance. A benchmark can help tremendously.
- Strategy Execution offers new chances for creating competitive advantage. Make sure you are the first in line to fully exploit the opportunity.

And the answer is? 'A new mathematical enigma: performance 0+0=8'.

The title refers to individual and organisational performance alignment. Alone, each cycle doesn't offer the organisation any value. Connected, they do.

"In a 4x100-metre relay race, one runner starts before the other, but in the end it's the sum of the four runners that determines performance"

CHAPTER II

You should be in the #1 spot

"Strategy Execution is the responsibility that makes or breaks executives"
– Alan Branche and Sam Bodley-Scott,
Implementation

"A strategy, even a great one, doesn't implement itself"

Living high in the mountain is an old guru renowned throughout the valley for his wisdom. One day, two young men decide to put the guru to the test. They catch a small bird in the forest at the foot of the mountain before climbing it. *En route*, they agree that they will hide the small bird behind their backs, then ask the guru whether it is dead or alive. If he says the bird is dead, they will open their hands and let the bird fly away. If he says the bird is alive, they will squeeze it in their hands to kill it. Either way, the guru will be proved wrong.

After days of trekking, they finally arrive at the top of the mountain. Standing before the guru, they ask: *"Do you know what we have behind our backs?"* The guru looks at the ground, strokes his long white beard and says: *"A small bird."* They then ask: *"Is the bird dead or alive?"*. Again the guru looks at the ground. After several minutes, he slowly raises his head and replies: *"Whether the bird lives or dies is up to you."*

I read this great story in Robin Speculand's first book *Bricks to*

Bridges, where he uses the story to stress the following point: ultimately, it's the responsibility (and choice) of the manager whether a strategy comes to life or dies.

The following chapter will expand on this crucial and central Strategy Execution role that a manager must play in order to get the performance delivered.

Are you a strategy tourist?

Let me start by reassuring you: the chances that you are a strategy tourist are close to zero. You are proving you are interested in getting things done by reading this action-oriented book. (Unless, of course, you have mistaken this book for something completely different).

But I'm sure you do *know* a strategy tourist.

Most likely you know plenty of them, since strategy tourists – those managers who lack the motivation, skills and knowledge to turn a strategy into performance – can be found in abundance in most organisations.

They are easily recognisable by the following characteristics:
- They love big words to make themselves sound more important.
- Their power drive is much larger than their achievements drive.
- They use expensive consultants for everything they do.
- They like to restart a new strategy exercise every year as while it's hard to define a strategy, it's even harder to stick to it rigorously and take the time to move it forwards.
- And yes, they are somewhat lazy.

I call the opposite of a strategy tourist a Strategy Execution hero. An individual dedicated to performance and to getting things done. You can find them in all disciplines but they do share the same competences, traits and beliefs. I'm sure you also know some.

Figure 3. A strategy tourist versus a Strategy Execution hero.

Strategy tourist ← → Strategy Execution hero	
• PowerPoint fanatic	• From PowerPoint to practice
• Do as I say, not as I do	• Actions speak louder than words
• We need to start from scratch	• Let's see what works
• I'm too important to focus on execution	• Execution is my priority

Strategy Execution and the leadership challenge

When I teach a Strategy Execution master class, I am often asked the question: 'What's the link between Strategy Execution and leadership?'.

My short answer is quite simple: Strategy Execution is a leadership essential. Or in other words, a good leader is also a good executioner. Being a great leader means being great at execution.

My long answer includes an animated group discussion of a selection of the following statements that I strongly believe in. (As I'm not here to discuss these in detail, you might want to find a partner to discuss them further).

The 12 Strategy Execution leadership statements:

1. Strategy Execution isn't something *others* are doing while you are working on something more important.
2. Your Strategy Execution role is part of your overall leadership role.
3. A good leader is a strategist *as well as* an implementer. It's not a question of either/or.
4. Most managers find it easier to define a new strategy than it is to implement the existing one.
5. Execution is part of your management job. It may sound boring, but nevertheless it is your job.
6. Don't mix execution with tactics.

7. Strategy Execution demands effort across all levels of the organisation. It's not just a lower-level task.
8. Most managers have been trained to plan, not execute.
9. Actions speak louder than words. Avoid managers with the motto 'Do as I say, not as I do'.
10. Managers play a crucial role in executing strategy. They contribute content, are the links between organisational levels, and act as performance role models.
11. Strategy remains a paper exercise without managers taking the right actions and fulfilling their roles.
12. If you play a leading role in your organisation, you need to put the right processes in place to ensure that all managers in your company become performance heroes. This is a challenge in itself.

The manager: a hero in a movie with many actors

Strategy Execution isn't a one-man show. It's a blockbuster movie, involving both business and support functions across various divisions, departments and teams. Each team member has a specific role to play, and it takes every member's contribution – collectively – to win.

And the manager needs to be the lead – the one in the limelight and in the thick of the action.

Figure 4. The manager in a central execution role

Strategy updates and help with strategy cascade or communication with the **strategy office**

Project prioritisation, resource allocation and status updates with the **PMO**

Budget allocation both for regular business and project budgets in collaboration with the **finance department**

MANAGER

Coordination of business support for IT projects with the **IT department**

Individual objective setting, coaching, evaluation and development of direct reports based on guidelines from the **HR department**

Aligning actions with **other departments**

PERFORMANCE TAKEAWAYS

- Strategy Execution isn't a game you play alone. There are numerous players from several departments involved.
- The managers, however, are the key players in the execution challenge. They contribute content, are the links between organisational levels, and act as performance role models.
- This makes Strategy Execution a part of a manager's role. In fact, it's a crucial building block – a leadership essential.
- Unfortunately, and for many reasons, some managers – the strategy tourists – see Strategy Execution as something others should do while they are working on something 'more important'.
- Don't make that mistake. Take on your implementation responsibility and become a Strategy Execution hero.

And the answer is? 'You should be in the #1 spot'.
Strategy Execution is all about people getting things done. And it's the manager who should take the lead.

How to turn your company into a holiday retreat for strategy tourists:
– You launch a new strategy exercise every six months.
– You stimulate power play.
– You don't punish low performers.
– Your promotion policy is based on 'who knows who'.
– You put everyone in a silo and clearly communicate that everyone outside the silo is considered less valuable and not worth talking to.

PART 2

ACT WITHIN THE 8

CHAPTER III

Challenge 1:
Aim:
Can you reach 245?

"In life, as in football, you won't go far unless you know
where the goalposts are"
– Arnold H. Glasgow

"The reason most people never reach their goals is that
they don't define them, or ever seriously consider them as
believable or achievable. Winners can tell you where they
are going, what they plan to do along the way, and who
will be sharing the adventure with them"
– Denis Watley

"No goal commitment equals no performance,
whatever else you try"

On 6 May 1954, Roger Bannister lined up for the race of his life. With a crosswind of 15-to-25mph (approx 24-to-32kph), the weather conditions that day were far from ideal. But nevertheless, he wrote history when he crossed the finishline three minutes and 59.4 seconds later. In fact, the breaking of the four-minute mile was so significant, that it was named by *Forbes* as one of the greatest athletic achievements of all time.

For years, it was widely believed impossible for any human to run 1609 metres in under four minutes. Even more so, physiologists of those times actually considered it dangerous to the health of any athlete who attempted it. The achievement of the four-minute mile was, until that historic day, considered a goal beyond human reach.

But when Bannister smashed the elusive four-minute mile, he also destroyed a psychological barrier. Other runners saw the goal within their grasp and, within three years of Bannister's momentous run, by the end of 1957, 16 other athletes had also run a sub-four-minute mile.

So how did Bannister do it?

He approached the task scientifically, set himself a rigid training schedule and broke down the overall goal into smaller, seemingly more feasible ones. Once set, they were quickly achieved: seven straight half-miles at an average time of 2:03, 10 straight quarter-miles at an average of 58.9, three-quarters of a mile in 2:59.8, and a half-mile in 1:54.

Successful people tend to have one thing in common: they are all extremely goal-oriented. Read any biography or article about a successful person and it will probably include a section about goal setting and how it helped them to improve their performance.

The corporate world has also widely adopted individual goal setting, or objective setting, as it is more widely known. But all too often, the process has unfortunately derailed into a 'once-a-year', formal, template-driven activity; a *pro-forma* exercise between a manager and team members, scheduled merely to comply with corporate HR policy.

And that's a shame. Because goal setting is one of the keys to Strategy Execution success. It's the final step in your strategy cascade. And it fuels the motivation of the individuals who adopt small pieces of your corporate strategy and transform them into desired performance. Successfully achieved, individual objective setting is a Strategy Execution booster.

Let's take a journey in this third chapter to the essence of goal-setting science and see how it can help you to achieve superior performance.

What you can learn from 100 goal-setting studies with 40,000 individuals

Did you know that the goal-setting theory is one of the most scientifically valid and useful theories in organisational science?

The positive results of setting objectives within the world of work are widely supported by substantial research – more than 100 scientific studies involving 40,000 participants from different industries. And these figures don't even include any goal-setting research that took place in the world of sport.

The research revealed some fascinating results. Reflect on the following:

1. Working *with* goals generally increases performance versus *not* working with goals.

2. Goals *directly* affect performance by steering what people pay attention to and how long and hard they work:
   - Goals direct our attention and effort towards goal-relevant activities and away from goal-irrelevant activities.
   - Goals have an energising function and make us work harder.
   - Goals make us more persistent. This results in us working more thoroughly.

3. Goals *indirectly* affect performance by motivating people to discover and utilise task strategies which will facilitate goal achievement:
   - People will automatically draw on a repertoire of skills they have previously used in a related context and apply them to crack the current challenge.
   - People will engage in deliberate planning to develop strategies that will enable them to attain their goals.

4. *Difficult* goals, when accepted, result in a higher level of performance than those of easy goals.

5. *Specific* goals work better than non-specific goals. That is, people perform better with clear stated goals rather than other types such as 'do your best' or 'work hard'.

6. If people face a task they find very complex, use *learning goals* instead of performance goals to improve overall performance. Why?

Because performance goals can make people so anxious that they fail to systematically look for solution strategies and learn what is effective.

7. The stronger the goal commitment, the higher the likelihood of success. Goal commitment increases when the goal is considered important and achievable.

"We tend to think that, in a traditional organisation, people are producing results because management wants results, but the essence of a high-quality organisation is people producing results because they want the results. It's puzzling we find that hard to understand, that if people are really enjoying, they'll innovate, they'll take risks, they'll have trust with one another because they are really committed to what they're doing and it's fun"
– Peter Senge

---

8. People with a high self-efficacy – a task-specific self-confidence – are more committed to assigned goals, find and use better task strategies to attain them, and respond more positively to negative feedback than do people with low self-efficacy.
9. Self-confidence can be improved by providing adequate training, by role modelling and by using persuasive communication.
10. Regular feedback on their goal progression improves people's performance.
11. Incentives shouldn't discourage risk taking, such as striving for near impossible goals.
12. Goal setting doesn't work when the reward mechanism is inappropriate.

The six secret success factors for best-in-class individual objective setting

Setting challenging and motivational goals is one of the best ways of improving performance – yours, your team's or even that of the entire organisation.

Let the goal-setting theory be your starting point. And once you've covered the basics, you can take your goal setting to the next level by applying the following six success factors:

Success factor 1: Don't break the strategy chain

Setting individual objectives isn't an isolated exercise. In fact, it's the final step in a series of events, all aimed at dividing the strategy into smaller parts. The sum of your individual objectives is your strategic action plan at the minutest level of detail.

In order to make it all add up, the relationship with the next level up is crucial. Without it, the organisational value is completely lost and could result in great sounding objectives which don't support your company strategy.

Here are some practical tips:

- *Make sure you understand the overall strategy.* If you don't, you won't be able to break it down. If things are not clear, it's your responsibility to take action. Don't blame your boss or someone else for not understanding the strategy.
- *Make sure you have a good understanding of the objectives defined on the organisational level above you.* These will serve as your framework.
- *Spend time communicating the strategy to your team.* It will help them to understand the relationship of their objectives to the overall strategy and the importance of their contribution. It will also increase their commitment towards their own goals.
- *Visualise the link between lower- and higher-level objectives.* Use a simple spreadsheet to connect the individual objectives with the higher-level goals.
- *Take responsibility to align objectives across hierarchical levels.* Take ownership to connect lower-level goals with yours and make certain yours fit with the next level up. Don't expect others to do it for you.

Success factor 2: Make sure it all adds up

Imagine you are the manager of an IT department comprised of 30 people, of whom eight are project managers, 19 project members and three support staff. You discover, via an internal audit, that only 73 percent of your projects deliver results on time and within budget. The main reason: poor project management.

You ask HR to find a good project management skills course and, being a good performance management scholar, give all eight project managers the following SMART objective: to take a two-day project management course in the following three months.

How great are your chances of attaining a better score on your next project delivery audit?

Pretty low, wouldn't you say? And that's not because the objective itself is wrong but because other objectives are missing to complement this one. In other words, the lower-level objective of sending your eight project managers on a two-day course, won't be enough to achieve your overall goal of improving the project delivery on time and on budget.

 Performance tip. Think about these mathematics for a minute. If you concentrate on only 50 percent of the objectives of the level above each time that you descend one hierarchical step, only 12.5 percent of your strategy will be covered by individual objectives after three cascade steps. And most organisations with 60 employees or more have at least three cascading steps. A large organisation easily has seven or more.

Always ask yourself the following question: 'Would I bet my own money on this combination of goals to reach the one above?'. If the answer is no, you still have some work to do.

Here are two actions you might want to consider:

1. What other goals can you add to increase the likelihood of success? Make a list. Rank all actions, starting with the one you think has the most impact on the realisation of your overall goal.

2. Try to reformulate the existing objectives.

So to sum up, evaluate not only *if* an individual objective contributes to the overall goal, but also question if the contribution is *large enough*. If not, take action.

Success factor 3: Don't be too SMART

What does the 'T' stand for in SMART? Is it 'Time-based' or is it...?

When I talk to managers, I often feel that goal setting has been downgraded to a 'using the SMART technique' drill. The essence has been lost. The acronym is well-known but few understand the real dynamics of goal setting and the added value for the successful implementation of a strategy. Most managers are clueless and thousands of company money is spent on training to reinforce this ignorance.

So does this mean that the SMART model is ineffective in today's working world? Not at all. It still has its advantages – it's recognised by most managers and is a great *aide memoire* for goal setting. Just be careful it doesn't become a goal in itself.

Success factor 4: Don't assume too quickly that someone is motivated

As you know, commitment is crucial to the success of individual objective setting. No commitment means no performance, whatever else you try. So while most managers focus only on the objectives, you want to focus on the objectives *and* the other person in the room, obtaining that crucial commitment.

But be careful. Peter Senge, author of the best-seller *The Fifth Discipline*, believes that *"Ninety percent of the time, what passes for commitment is compliance"*. In other words, you might think you have that very important goal commitment in the bag, but in reality, you don't. You only have something that resembles the real thing.

> *"Real commitment means doing everything in your power to get things done."*

Peter developed an effective seven-point scale to categorise employee reactions, only one of which is Commitment. It's a great tool for identifying 'non-commitment' behaviour. And you can use your findings to create an open dialogue to gain true commitment:

1. *Commitment:* wants it, will make it happen.
2. *Enrolment:* wants it, will do whatever can be done within the 'spirit of the law'.
3. *Genuine Compliance*: sees the benefits of the vision. Good soldier, follows the 'letter of the law'.
4. *Formal Compliance:* on the whole sees the benefits of the vision. Does what is expected and no more. 'Pretty good' soldier.
5. *Grudging Compliance:* does not see the benefits of the vision, but also doesn't want to lose job. Does enough of what's expected, but also lets it be known that s/he is not onboard.
6. *Non-Compliance:* does not see the benefits of the vision and will not do what's expected. 'I won't do it, you can't make me'.
7. *Apathy:* neither for or against the vision. No interest. No energy. 'Is it five o'clock yet?'.

Success factor 5: Focus on getting the leadership objectives right

Most people find it difficult to define high-quality leadership objectives. In fact, almost all managers I know find it much easier to define 'hard' business objectives than 'soft' ones.

But instead of putting in the extra effort required to get them right, they take the easy way out and end up with leadership objectives such as 'go to leadership training', 'organise more communication sessions' or 'work on your management skills'.

So what's the magic trick to define those leadership objectives? Here are just a few that will help you get the job done:

- *Think and talk behaviour.* Describe and discuss suitable behaviour – and equally or even more importantly, what doesn't fit.
- *Compare behaviour.* Do you know somebody who has the right leadership behaviour? Use them as an example in your discussion.
- *Keep it simple.* Competency dictionaries and leadership models often provided are way too detailed and won't serve your purpose. Don't try too hard!
- *Don't overdo the measuring part.* People with SMART training under their belts have been taught to make every objective measurable. But participants need a discussion and feedback, not a mathematical formulae.

 Performance download 3. Interesting leadership resources.

Two final comments:
- Most people are interested in self-development and time and effort invested in helping them define high-quality leadership objectives increases motivation.
- Discussing leadership objectives will take the working relationship to another level and often opens the door for performance coaching.

Success factor 6: Don't let a template ruin an important exercise

Ideally you shouldn't need to worry about templates. But since the world isn't ideal, you might be faced with a highly complex and user-unfriendly objective-setting document.

But don't let a poor-quality document affect your professionalism. Don't allow your meeting to disintegrate into a 'we have to fill in this template for corporate reasons' exercise. This won't do justice to either you or your colleagues.

Keep the quality standards as high as possible. Start with a blank sheet of paper if it helps. You can always transfer the results of your meeting onto the template later.

And don't forget to tell those in charge that the document isn't fit for the job. If they are smart, they will get to work.

What your organisation can do to improve individual goal setting

By now, you should have a better insight into goal-setting dynamics and learnt six valuable lessons to take your individual objective setting to new heights. Let's now have a look at what an organisation can do to build a best-in-class individual objective-setting practice:

Tip 1: Promote the benefits, not the mechanics. The goal-setting theory is fascinating. It's one of the cornerstones of modern management and gives great insight into human behaviour. It should also be basic knowledge for any manager taking objective setting seriously. Don't let SMART training be your organisation's best goal-setting effort. Explain why goal setting helps your company realise its strategy. Aim for the bigger picture, promote the overall goal-setting benefits and help your managers look way beyond the mechanics.

Tip 2: Keep it simple. Make your goal-setting tools and templates manager-oriented. Keep them simple and easy to find and you will go a long way. There are several guidelines in Chapter 6 that will help you make small or large improvements.

Tip 3: Set goals for goal setting. Give clear and challenging goals on goal setting to everyone – employees, managers, the executive team – as well as those responsible for the individual goal-setting process within the organisation – in most cases HR. The initiative will promote goal-setting, increase goal-setting performance and serve as best-practice.

Tip 4: Develop the necessary skills. Setting high-quality individual objectives for yourself or others is an art. There are so many factors to take into account including the organisational context, the strategy, individual capabilities and a fair amount of psychology.

But the consequence is that the overall goal-setting quality in your organisation largely depends on the individual's ability to operate within the goal-setting process.

Make sure everyone involved knows exactly what's expected of them (Tip 3) and provide adequate development opportunities. Look at Chapter 8 for practical development tips and guidelines.

Tip 5: Build a feedback culture. Feedback increases performance. But in order to maximise the potential advantage, you need a culture that fosters feedback opportunities and stimulates learning from them.

 Performance download 4. How to give effective feedback – tips.

Tip 6: Make sure those at the top also have individual objectives. An obvious one... but one not always applied. And don't forget the leadership objectives.

Tip 7: Don't try to fit everything into one meeting. Traditionally, managers hold an annual formal meeting with those who report directly to them in order to set objectives for the coming year. But all too often, this meeting gets packed with other topics such as future career steps, mobility and talent management. And the result? Poor-quality individual objectives and lack of commitment.

Don't ask your managers to cram all those subjects into one meeting. They won't have time to cover any topic properly. Keep the objective-setting meeting for what it is meant to be: set high-quality, agreed upon (commitment!) objectives.

Tip 8: Monitor the individual objective quality. Individual objective setting is crucial to Strategy Execution success – and you want to keep an eye on things that are important. Keep the quality of the individual objectives on the radar and take corrective action when necessary. Here is a three-step quality check that can be actioned on any level, whether company-wide, business unit, department or team.

- *Quality check 1: Verify fit with strategy.* Each objective – even at the lowest level of your organisation – should be linked to your strategy. I discovered that, even after a well-implemented strategy cascade, 25-to-35 percent of the individual objectives do not support the actual strategy. They are often survivors from the previous strategy, personal pet objectives or built on strategy misunderstandings. Make sure you put a process in place to go after them and nuke them!

- *Quality check 2: Verify the quality of the objective.* There's no need to check all objectives. Your objective is not to improve each one, but to get a realistic feeling for the general quality and the most common quality issues.

  Focus on the objectives from senior management as they are the basis for the rest of the organisation. Aim for a 15 percent sample for the levels below.

- *Quality check 3: Measure satisfaction.* This is your commitment indicator. You know that the output of a good individual objective-setting meeting is more than a list of high-quality objectives linked with strategy. It's also about the acceptance of these objectives. Remember: reality shows that a tough discussion during the meeting doesn't automatically translate into a bad score. On the contrary, if you analyse the bad scores, it's often because there was no discussion at all.

  And one more thing: you don't need to aim for a perfect score as there will always be individuals unhappy with the exercise, no matter what you do. But you do want to end up above 75 percent.

Tip 9: Build and use a dashboard. I am a big fan of a dashboard covering all three quality criteria that offer a multi-year perspective. Even break it down by business unit, department or team and make interesting comparisons.

Or benchmark yourself with other companies!

The results are a great starting point to develop a targeted action plan aimed at increasing individual objective-setting maturity in your organisation.

A view on Strategy Execution by Michael Smith, Vice President Group Strategy and Planning, Coca-Cola North America

What do you consider to be the most important Strategy Execution challenge for an executive team?

A senior team has many challenges but one of the most important is to agree on the time window when discussing strategy and its execution. You want all members to discuss these important topics with the same time frame (window) in mind. This is crucial as each time horizon has its specific challenges.

Let me explain about the three strategy windows I see and give you some examples of the differences between them.

1. One-year outlook

This time frame demands a leadership team to be focusing very much on the execution of the strategy. The team should have *a shared picture of what success looks like* for the different business areas (brands, channels, consumers, customers ...).

And it needs to be a detailed view as the one-year time frame needs to be concrete with regards to the execution of the strategy. Don't be satisfied with the perception that everyone is aligned, you need to be 100 percent sure.

In my experience a good way to achieve this crucial alignment is to define *common execution metrics* to monitor success. When you have a shared picture of what success looks like, and agreed upon metrics to monitor the progress towards this goal, your team is in an excellent position to make choices and achieve its objectives.

When things are not going as planned, this common view of success and its metrics will help the executive team to evaluate if problems are related either to the quality of the strategy or to its execution. And it will make a huge difference for an organisation if the leadership decides to change the strategy versus a modification of the execution of the existing one.

2. Three-year outlook

The second time horizon is the three-year outlook. The leadership agenda will be different. It will be not so much focused on a clear short- term view of success but on building *core capabilities to sustainably capture growth*. It's about, or should be about, identifying those capabilities – such as the right consumer-driven portfolio, customer marketing or other go-to-market business models – you need to develop as an system to maintain/develop your competitive advantage.

I'm a strong believer in having this discussion within this three-year time frame as it *takes time* for an organisation to further develop an existing capability or develop a new one. So start well ahead and avoid having these crucial capability discussions when you only have one year to master them. In most cases, in my view, that would not be realistic.

The key three-year Strategy Execution question is: 'What does it take to extract value in identified (the identification is done in your long-term plan) profit areas?'. In other words, 'What are the capabilities I need to develop in the coming two-to-three years to realise my long-term vision in a sustainable way?'. And the answer will be to either further develop one or more existing capabilities or start developing new ones.

And again you need to define and agree on *metrics to measure your progress*. These metrics need to help you decide – when needed – whether to continue to build certain capabilities or shift to others. There is no point in building capabilities for a strategy that is no longer valid.

3. Five-year outlook

The third and final time horizon that merits a specific discussion is the long-term outlook. The time frame will *vary from industry to industry*. Five years in the consumer industry is an eternity for example, whereas in the car industry it would be a mid-term horizon.

But no matter what the industry, it's important to have a *separate agenda* and a moment with the leadership team to talk about these long-term aspirations.

These discussions will fuel the capability discussions and help to screen crucial investment decisions. The long-term is a yardstick for everything else that happens in the organisation and crucial for long-term success.

What Strategy Execution advice would you give to an ambitious manager?

Strategy Execution is an important skill for any manager. Based on my experience, here's my advice:

1. **Steer the frontline.** Make sure you are able to take a complex strategy and turn it into three-to-five priorities for the frontline. Not everything can be important. And it's your job to take a decision and guide the people in the field.

2. **Develop a sixth sense.** Superior results demand a great strategy and great execution. Make sure you develop both skills. But maybe even more importantly, develop a sixth sense to know when your strategy is good enough to move to execution.

3. **Stay in touch.** Make sure you are – and stay – in touch with the execution of your strategy. It will quite likely go wrong if you don't keep in touch.

4. **Learn to allocate the problem.** When a problem arises, you need to be able to evaluate if the problem is related to a bad strategy or a bad execution. I see quite a lot of managers changing their strategy too quickly when things are not working out as they had planned.

After a closer look, the strategy is often okay but the quality of its execution isn't. So make sure you are able to allocate issues and don't kill your strategy too quickly.

5. ***Be honest about your ability to build capabilities***. As I mentioned before, it takes time to develop or build new capabilities. History shows that you don't build capabilities overnight. It takes time before a specific capability becomes a competitive advantage.

    Based on my experience, managers are also too optimistic and try to combine capability building and execution too much in the same time frame. You need to ask yourself 'What can I really expect from my organisation … do they have the capacity to both execute against my short-term plan while simultaneously building capabilities?'.

    So, be realistic from the start and avoid having to come back on something you said or planned at the start, secretly knowing it wasn't realistic in the first place.

6. ***Aim for continuity***. People in the field are looking for continuity. Your strategy should not constantly change. And if you do change something, spend the necessary time explaining why. And make sure you communicate if there is a change in the strategy or a shift in the execution.

7. ***Define and agree upon the right execution metrics.*** Strategy Execution isn't an exact science. And things can, and will go wrong from time-to-time. If you only use lagging indicators, it's too late to see what is going wrong. So make sure you have put in place, and agreed upon, a set of leading metrics that predict future success.

    This approach will also reduce finger pointing between departments when things do go wrong. We all know the following corporate saying 'People in the field did not execute' versus the local branch indicating that 'This was not the right approach for our market' and the frontline responding 'You gave me too much so I could not prioritise'.

    So look and agree upfront on those six or seven execution metrics and track/discuss them consistently.

8. **Introduce a Strategy Execution approach that fits your company.** I believe your Strategy Execution approach should depend on the speed at which your environment is changing. In an environment that is changing slowly, the execution focus should be on consistency and productivity to create a better alignment than the competition. In a fast-changing environment, you need to put a flexible execution process in place that can follow your innovation speed.

Based on your experience, what's a classic Strategy Execution mistake?

The first thing that comes to mind is strategy communication and strategy cascading, two crucial elements of Strategy Execution that are closely linked. The overall message needs to be *consistently communicated and cascaded across all the hierarchical lines*. And you will probably agree that this creates problems in many organisations. If your strategy was called a horse, many organisations will end up with a zebra after cascading it to the troops. And while a zebra might still be okay, you definitely don't want to end up with a chicken.

So, to avoid these classical mistakes, make sure your organisation has a *flexible, high-quality cascade and communication approach* – whether it's the Balanced Scorecard, OGSM or other – to make sure that the horse stays a horse.

Looking at Strategy Execution from a 'strategy department' point of view, what are important topics for you?

I find it very important that a candidate for a senior strategy position has had *a fair amount of Strategy Execution experience*. This helps to put strategy into a different perspective. Managers with vertical careers in strategy departments alone risk being too academic and fail to evaluate the execution challenges in the right way. So horizontal moves are a must.

And I like to stress the importance of *a partnership between the finance and strategy department* in order to make sure content and numbers reinforce each other.

PERFORMANCE TAKEAWAYS

- Individual objective setting is the final step of your strategy cascade and therefore a crucial ingredient for successful Strategy Execution.
- Setting challenging goals that motivates is one of the best things you can do to improve performance – yours, your team's or even that of an entire organisation.
- Gain insight into the goal-setting theory, a fascinating cornerstone of modern organisational development.
- Use tested ideas from the goal-setting research to get your objective-setting basics right.
- Take your goal setting to the next level by applying the following six success factors:
  1. Keep the strategy chain intact.
  2. Make sure that all objectives add up to the objective one level above.
  3. Don't let the SMART technique be your one and only goal setting wisdom.
  4. Don't assume too quickly that someone is motivated.
  5. Focus on getting the leadership objectives right.
  6. Don't let a template ruin an important exercise.
- Create an environment where goal setting can thrive.
- Benchmark the quality of your objective-setting process, build an action plan and beat your competitors.

And the answer is? 'Can you reach 245?'.
The title is a reference to the world record of Javier Sotomayor. He jumped more than 2.45 metres at an athletics meeting in Salamanca in 1993. It's the longest-standing world record in the history of the men's high jump. You can watch Sotomayor's record jump on YouTube.

We can all be inspired by the world of sport, a world that thrives on goal setting. Athletes visualise a goal and train for years and years to reach what is pictured in their minds. Each world record becomes a new goal in the everlasting search for top performance.

I find goal setting fascinating. It looks deceptively easy on the surface but covers a variety of human psychology. I also believe setting goals and chasing after them is one of the best things you can do for yourself. It provides your life and work with meaning, purpose and structure. It contributes to overall happiness and success.

Are you getting all the benefits from goal setting?

Think about it before moving on to the next chapter.

CHAPTER IV

Challenge 2: Communicate: 121, 1210 and 12100 or more

"Like a human being, a company has to have an internal communication mechanism, a 'nervous system', to coordinate its actions"
– Bill Gates, co-founder Microsoft

"The result of bad communication is a disconnection between strategy and execution"
– Chuck Martin, former Vice President IBM

"Look beyond the send button and shift your focus to the receiving end"

Afew weeks ago, I was on the phone with Michael Smith, VP Group Strategy and Planning at Coca-Cola North America, discussing different Strategy Execution challenges. We were talking about strategy communication and he made me laugh with a funny analogy. He said: *"If your strategy is called 'horse', you might get away when it's called 'zebra' after you're done cascading your strategy across the organisation – but you definitely don't want to end up with a chicken!"*

Besides making me laugh, it reminded me of a game I used to play as a kid. You have probably played it as well. It's most commonly called 'Telephone'. You secretly whisper a phrase into your neighbour's ear who then passes on the message they have heard to the next in line. At the end, the final message will most likely bear little or no resemblance to the original, because of the cumulative effect of mistakes along the line.

One of the lessons this game taught us as children was how simple it is for messages to become corrupted by unclear, indirect communication. But how did we forget the lessons?

The communication of strategy and its execution comes in different shapes and forms: from individual conversations during objective setting over group interactions around the Balanced Scorecard, and from intranet postings to writing a memo regarding a strategy shift.

But they all serve one purpose: to get the strategy into the *heads, hearts* and *hands* of the people:

- *Heads*: You want everyone to *understand* the strategy.
- *Hearts*: You want everyone to be *motivated* by the strategy.
- *Hands*: You want everyone to *take action to get things done.*

Communication of the strategy and its execution is an essential, on-going component of your implementation efforts. And although some elements might seem trivial and simplistic on the surface as everyone can communicate to some degree, the reality shows that it demands substantial skill and knowledge to communicate the relevant information to the desired person that results in the required action.

So the question isn't so much *if* you communicated but *how well*. In other words, don't focus on the question 'Was my message communicated?' but rather on 'Was my message effective?'. Look beyond the send button and shift your focus to the receiving end.

This chapter will help you evaluate the quality of the various communication methods you have at your disposal and provide you with tips and tricks to improve your strategy communication skills.

> Get your strategy into the heads, hearts and hands of your people!
> - Heads: You want everyone to understand the strategy.
> - Hearts: You want everyone to be motivated by the strategy.
> - Hands: You want everyone to take action to get things done.

Building pyramids – strategic thinking demystified

Why am I talking about pyramids you might wonder?

Apart from the fact that pyramids have been referred to as one of the 'world's greatest treasures of all times', they are also the visual image that Barbara Minto uses in her fantastic book about communication called *The Pyramid Principle*. But before talking about this further, let me first tell you something important.

Something happens to people when they start writing a business document that they want you to read – be it a Word document, slide show or email. They concentrate so hard on getting their ideas in writing, using their own mental models, that they forget about you, the reader.

And nobody likes to be ignored, right?

We all use mental models to structure our thinking. It's part of how our brains work. It is necessary. Without automatic mental framing, you wouldn't be able to function correctly.

So where's the problem, you might ask?

Writers who focus on themselves instead of their readers put their own mental model down on paper. Want to know why?

Because it's the easiest way.

"I have made this letter longer than usual because I lack the time to make it shorter" said Blaise Pascal. A perfect illustration of the point I want to make. Allowing your thoughts to gush out from your own perspective without taking the time to deconstruct them and represent them in a neutral context, is the fastest way of writing, even if the finished text is twice the length it needs to be.

Leaving your mental model behind and getting your thoughts on neutral territory demands a big effort, but one that will become easier with practice. And that extra effort will result in people enjoying your work and contemplating your ideas, since you took the time to de-frame the message. And isn't that what you are after?

Putting your strategy down on paper can be a disheartening experience. But the better you are able to structure your own thinking, the easier and more quickly you will finish. And this is true for all communication methods. So whether you are preparing a one-to-one strategy communication, a speech for your team or a strategy document, remember to structure it first and write it later.

There are several helpful tips in the training document or for more in-depth guidelines, refer to Barbara Minto's book which you can find on Amazon.

 Performance download 5. *The Pyramid Principle –* training module.

Boost your one-to-one communication skills

Don't you find it surprising that most people don't pay much attention to the person they are talking to?

In fact, as with writing, some focus so hard on *what* they're saying that they completely neglect *who* they are talking to.

A shame, because the interaction itself determines if the message has been taken onboard and been correctly understood. So make sure you establish a connection first and then focus on the message you want to give.

There are several techniques to help improve your ability to make a connection. I'm a big fan of dynamic models; techniques that enable you to shift gears during communication to obtain and maintain the optimal connection with your counterpart. Static models can give you valuable insights into human communication behaviour, but they aren't very useful on a day-to-day level.

So for the purpose of executing your strategy, I would opt for the dynamic ones. Spend some time selecting which works best for you. It's better to master one model than to have a general feeling for 10 different ones.

My all-time favourite is the communication model with four interaction levels. To learn how to use it, you can download the training material.

 Performance download 6. A great communication model – training module.

Become an author: put your thoughts on paper and make them fun to read

Wouldn't you agree that writing a novel holds a special kind of magic?

We can all imagine the lonesome soul sitting in a secret wooden cabin, working on his masterpiece. One mind bringing dozens of characters to life destined to enter the minds of thousands of readers all over the world. I, for one, have little trouble imagining Michael Connelly or Lee Child, two of my favourite fiction writers, bringing Harry Bosch and Jack Reacher to life to solve great mysteries.

Our writing however is different. It has nothing to do with heroes or great mysteries. Our writing aims to communicate ideas, a strategy, a plan – but most of all, it needs to motivate and trigger action. In other words, your aim isn't to construct great prose but to convey your great ideas.

And the effort to achieve this may be less than you imagine. With a few simple tricks, you can structure your ideas and entice people into your words by boosting your writing skills.

To help you achieve this goal, I've collected some little-known secrets from famous copywriters. In the second part, you will also discover the tools to turn your PowerPoint presentations into works of art.

But be careful, once you get started you might get hooked... and even end up as an author!

"Body language can't save you when someone is reading your strategy document"

Performance tip. Writing is an essential skill for any manager with ambitions to be a Strategy Execution champion. You won't always be there to explain, clarify or even defend your ideas, so your words will have to do the talking.

A few tricks of the copywriters' trade

You know what you want to say. You have structured your great strategic ideas into a logical structure. And now for the tricky bit. The writing!

Let's look at six proven tips to transform your current words into hypnotic writing.

- **Trick 1: Focus on the reader.** Most writers focus on themselves. What you want to do is focus on the reader. In other words, address their interests. Every sentence you write should mean something to them. As David Ogilvy, founder of one of the world's most successful marketing agencies, said: *"The reader's not an idiot, he's your husband"*. (Although this phrase might only work if you are happily married).

- **Trick 2: Ask questions.** What's the best way to hook in your reader? Do you have any ideas? Have you noticed what I'm doing? That's three in a row now. Have you figured it out yet? Questions are a great way to hook you, the reader, into the content. They tease your brain and create two-way interaction. It works, doesn't it?

- **Trick 3: Don't be blocked by the writer's block.** Starting to write can be the most difficult part, especially if you don't have a precise idea of the structure. If you are not sure about what to include in the introduction, don't let it delay you. Just start with the second paragraph and write the introduction at the end.

- **Trick 4: Separate writing from editing.** Don't aim for Shakespearean style sentences in your first draft. Write your first draft at lightning speed with the editing part of your brain turned off. Walk away from it for at least 24 hours. Then turn your editing brain back on and edit to perfection. Your work is done after a final spell-check and proofread.

If you have the time, you could spend some extra moments working on the structure before editing.

- **Trick 5: Include the benefits.** If you want people to take action, you need to offer them something in return. So make sure you answer the 'what's in it for me?' (read 'me = reader') question with great care.

- **Trick 6: Watch your language.**
  - Avoid overly technical words.
  - Keep your sentences short. Aim for an average of 16 words per sentence.
  - Don't use a fancy word when a simple one will do.
  - Don't use five words when one can say the same thing. Be concise!
  - Don't over-use the same words. Use a thesaurus if you need.
  - After editing, read it out loud. Awkward sentences and errors will stand out.

I don't have to tell you it takes time and lots of practice to become a skilled writer. Nobody becomes an author overnight. However, your business writing can improve significantly if you master the tips provided in this chapter. If you want to perfect your writing craft, you could have a look at some of the books on the following list.

 Performance download 7. Great books on writing – a list.

Make killer PowerPoint presentations to communicate your strategy

Remember the last time you were invited to a presentation that initially seemed quite interesting, but then turned out to be a real disappointment?

Endless slides with a font too small to read from where you sat, graphics that you couldn't quite grasp and a total absence of structure. And before you knew it, you were wondering what you wanted for dinner that evening.

The ability to create a relevant, structured and concise PowerPoint presentation is crucial. It's the number one method of communication in many companies.

And while it may seem easier to write and produce a good PowerPoint presentation than a full document, it's not. Let me tell you why.

A PowerPoint presentation gives you less space to present your ideas than a Word document (unless of course you relish challenging the eyesight of your audience or wish to bore them with a zillion slides). And less space demands more effort.

Most tips you find on the creation of PowerPoint presentations relate to the visuals, and while an essential part of any PowerPoint presentation, they are only one element.

As a former director of a large consulting company, I've seen thousands of PowerPoint presentations, made hundreds myself and taught others how to put them together. Here are some of the tricks I use and teach:

Tip 1: Get straight to the point. Don't wait until the end of your presentation to tell your audience your key message. You're not Agatha Christie, the greatest suspense-builder of all time. Your first slide should summarise the situation, explain the reason for the presentation, pose the question you'd like to answer and offer a summary of the answer itself.

Tip 2: Use a professional PowerPoint template. Make sure you have a PowerPoint template on your computer. Most companies have a standard but it might not completely suit your needs.

Tip 3: Each slide should have a topline. A topline is a phrase at the top of each page summarising the page content. Everything on that page needs to relate to the title. If it doesn't, either change your topline or adapt your content.

Performance tip. Copy all of your toplines onto a separate page. Collectively, they should provide your storyline. It needs to flow.

Tip 4: Use separation slides selectively. Only use separation slides when there are lots of slides. They are boring and should be avoided.

Tip 5: Size matters. How many people will be in the room at the same time to see your presentation? Twelve, 55 or 190?

If you present to a group of more than 50, the font size of the text will need to be at least 18pt, including that used on the graphs (the graphs are often forgotten).

If you can't increase it to 18pt, consider creating two versions – a headline-only version for your speech and a full version as the handout.

Tip 6: Spend extra time on your key slides. You should consider your key slides as marketing material. They need to look great and summarise the main points. Try to add visuals but avoid tables.

Re-use these slides in follow-up presentations or any other opportunity you get.

Tip 7: Select the right visuals. Make sure your visuals reinforce your message. When you make a comparison, your visual should also be about a comparison. Most people are lazy and just copy a table into their presentation. Ensure that your visuals match your content.

There's a great book called *Say It With Charts* by Gene Zelazny that has become a classic for strategy consultants worldwide. It covers all you need to make your presentations look great and maximise the effectiveness of the content.

Tip 8: Collect and develop visuals in downtime. Have a set of visuals ready that you can use when time is tight. Graphics can be particularly time-consuming, so it's good to have them pre-prepared. Get into the habit also of collecting slides you like and reproducing them in your template document.

Tip 9: Use visual indicators. They offer the reader an extra support – besides your titles – to follow the build-up of your document.

Tip 10: Use version numbers. You should do this especially when working with more than one on a presentation. Also indicate when something is final. I use the following convention: date_maintopic_subtopic_version ('f' if final). Add the code as a footer to your presentation.

Tip 11: Avoid making one point over two slides. When you see '(cont.)' written on a slide, you know that not enough thinking went into the presentation. Review your structure and either try to break-up the point into smaller topics or summarise and put it on one page.

Tip 12: Keep your storyline up-to-date. When you re-use the presentation after some time, make sure you have adapted its content to the current situation. You might want to consider drastically shortening certain parts or move others to the appendix.

Tip 13: Keep a balance between topics. Give each of your topics the same amount of slide space. You don't want 10 slides covering one point and two slides the second. It would over-complicate your presentation structure. Keep each block about the same size. If one of your topics becomes too elaborate, try and move some of the information to the appendix or divide the topic.

Tip 14: Use a summary slide. Depending on the situation and setting, this could either summarise or list the decisions to take. It's often the most challenging slide to produce. If there is a call for action, it's worthwhile spending some extra time thinking about its formulation. Make sure you know exactly what you want them to do. You might even want to test the formulation to see if it has the desired effect.

Inspire an audience

Some people like it but the majority don't. What am I referring to?

Talking in front of an audience. But as with all other skills, it's something you can learn. And while your skills increase, enjoyment also increases.

You can download a list with great tips. Let me just highlight two basic ones that helped me a lot when I started speaking to large groups a decade ago:

 Performance download 8. Improve your podium performance – tips.

- The first one I call 'Be a Tree'. Have you noticed the way most people shift uncomfortably from foot-to-foot when they stand in front of a group? They take small steps backwards and forwards, as if they want to start dancing but are afraid to do so. Meanwhile their hands don't move at all!

  You actually need to achieve the precise opposite. Your legs and feet shouldn't move – they are the tree trunk, firmly planted and immovable. Your arms are the twigs – they move freely in the wind (read 'your arm movement should reinforce your message').

  If you do want to move, do so deliberately. Move to another part of the room or podium. I call it replanting. One step forwards or backwards doesn't count. It has to be at least five.

- The second basic tip covers your facilitation style, using a facilitation model called 'The Facilitation Rainbow'. I learnt it quite a while ago when working for Arthur D. Little. I liked it a lot then and still do. In fact, I like it so much I teach it in one of my master classes and always use it to prepare for a group interaction, whether it's a keynote address, workshop or lecture.

  In a nutshell, the Rainbow model can help you pick the most suitable audience interaction for a specific situation. It's a scale (hence the name), ranging from telling modus to complete audience empowerment. And each interaction type demands different skills from the facilitator.

For more advanced speakers and group facilitators, I would recommend studying others. You can learn a lot by observing successful speakers in various situations. Let colleagues, clients or even TV news presenters inspire your communication.

Like to read a good book on the subject?

Check out *Success Secrets of the Motivational Superstars* by Michael Jeffreys, a highly reputable and classic book on the subject in which he has collected the top secrets of 15 high calibre motivational speakers.

Nineteen tips to improve strategy communication in your organisation

International research from Watson Wyatt confirms what communication adepts have advocated for years: organisations that excel in their internal communications also excel in their financial performance.

In fact, the study found that companies with highly effective communication practices have a 19 percent higher market premium, 57 percent higher shareholder returns over five years, and levels of employee engagement 4.5 times higher than their competitors.

As a strong believer in high-quality strategy communication, I am not surprised by these results. Successful Strategy Execution depends heavily on a thorough understanding of the strategy by everyone within the organisation. You can't implement what you don't understand. So if you want help turning your strategy into performance, you need a sound strategy communication; one that is clear, consistent, honest and inspirational. The more people you get onboard, the better your success rate. A simple logic, wouldn't you agree?

But where the logic is simple, the quality is often lacking. Most companies don't spend enough time communicating their strategy and when they do, the quality and effectiveness is dubious.

Be different. Make your strategy communication coherent and motivational. And transform it into an essential success component of your Strategy Execution.

Here are 19 simple but effective tips to get you on your way. You can also start with a strategy communication checklist.

Performance download 9. Evaluate the quality of your strategy communication – a checklist.

Tip 1: Don't rush. Don't use an *ad hoc* strategy selling approach for your new strategy, however tempting it might be. You gave your new strategy a lot of thought so take your time, take a step back and prepare a thorough, tailor-made strategy communication approach.

Tip 2: Avoid gold-plating. But you don't want to wait forever either. Don't delay your strategy communication for the sake of a perfect score. A 95 percent score is fine – as perfect communication doesn't actually exist.

Tip 3: Assure follow-up communication. Once you start communicating, keep the ball rolling. The follow-up communication is just as important, if not more so, than the launch. Think marketing. People need to hear things several times before it sinks in and becomes relevant.

Tip 4: Build a best-in-class strategy communication plan. As I have already pointed out, communicating a strategy isn't a one-off event. Successful strategy communication is a collection of consistent, well-planned activities across different channels, delivered by a team of individuals.

These activities need orchestration. Make sure you have a professional communication plan covering at least the first six months after the initial communication. Here's an example for downloading.

 Performance download 10. Build a professional strategy communication plan – 'how to' guide.

Tip 5: Use proven communication channels. You can communicate through a variety of channels – but using more or new channels doesn't automatically result in better communication. Your message might be new, but your communication channels needn't be.

Use the medium that has worked effectively in the past – the tried and tested. If, for example, you used team meetings to communicate important messages in the past, do so again.

You might want to consider doing something special for the strategy launch, but in general, it's best to stick to the communication channels everyone knows and trusts.

Tip 6: Use simple language. Your strategy might be a complex challenge but your words need to be kept simple. The words: 'To enhance our competitive position in growth markets and protect us against eroding margins and demand fluctuations, we are going to leverage our new distribution capabilities' might actually summarise your strategy, but won't create much excitement.

Tip 7: Involve a copywriter or the communications department – but do not hand over. It's smart to get a professional to craft your communication – but there is a risk. Your strategy message might come back over-simplified or with a tone of voice slightly off-beat. If you opt for professional support, make sure you stay in the driver's seat. Keep control of the message and tone of voice.

Tip 8: Inspire. Start with an inspiring vision to capture the imagination. Summarise the vision in an elevator pitch, enabling everyone to rephrase and reproduce it to friends and family. An inspiring vision will create a sense of ownership, commitment and energy among your people.

Tip 9: Give your strategy a face. Research shows that people remember first the form, then the colour and finally the text. Help employees remember your strategy by developing a catchy name and logo. It will boost recognition.

Tip 10: What's in it for me? That's the main question your audience will have on their minds. More specifically, they will be asking themselves: 'How will this new strategy influence my job in a positive or negative way'. Make sure you have an adequate answer. Remember: most strategy presentations don't score well on this point.

*Tip 11: **Get your managers on board.*** Managers are a crucial target group for your strategy communication since they are in the frontline, answering questions from concerned employees. They should be your strategy ambassadors, your word-of-mouth generals promoting the new strategy and its implementation.

Managers are crucial to the overall communication success and deserve special treatment but, in reality, most organisations don't even have a structured approach for reaching this target group. General messages in the internal newsletter, an uninspired mass communication or boring presentations in staff meetings, are usually as good as it gets.

Make sure you do it differently.

*Tip 12: **Work on the communication skills of the CEO.*** Unless you are the CEO, this could be a potentially tricky point. Not everyone is a top communicator with the charisma of Steve Jobs. But you might be amazed at how much communication can be improved by working on style, tone of voice, messaging and delivery.

So talk to your CEO and work on perfecting those skills. Remember that even a small improvement at the top makes a big difference at the bottom.

And if you find it difficult being the messenger, you can always show him/her this paragraph!

*Tip 13: **Treat your strategy as your core product.*** I'm often surprised to see companies demonstrating extreme professionalism when it comes to communicating a new product or service externally, but then failing miserably when it comes to communicating their strategy internally.

Why not apply some of that marketing expertise to boost your internal communication?

Treat your strategy as your future cash cow product, use the marketing skills available within the organisation and launch a professional campaign, as you would do for any other important product.

*Tip 14: **Make your launch event something to remember.*** You want people to talk about your strategy kick-off. But it doesn't have to be expensive to be effective. If you're moving to a new building for example, hold the event there.

Be creative.

Tip 15: Use a test group. Try-outs are great but most companies skip the test phase and go live without it. And that's a shame.

Organising a trial run with a real audience is a great way to assess your timing, poll for difficult questions and get valuable feedback.

Tip 16: Manage message consistency. This is particularly important within larger organisations as numerous managers will deliver the same strategy communication.

Take your time to get everyone up to speed. Just because someone heard your presentation once, doesn't mean they could deliver it in the same way.

Provide your standard presentation with extensive notes. Organise phone conferences to run through the presentation and notes and allow for plenty of time to answer questions.

You might also consider giving suggestions on tone of voice, tackling difficult questions and other elements that help to keep the message consistent.

Tip 17: Use direct marketing techniques for Q&As. Learn from marketers and address your people personally.

Capture the questions from a communication session. Translate them into a Q&A format and send a personal email with the answers a few days later to your target group. You can repeat this process several times adding new answers.

Tip 18: Include implementation information. Communicate the Strategy Execution process itself and the concrete role of the manager. This helps create the bigger picture. Some general questions you want to answer:

– What is Strategy Execution?
– Why is this so important for our company?

- What's expected from a manager?
- How can I improve my Strategy Execution skills?
- Where can I find the information I need?

You can hold a short brainstorming session to call out the more specific process questions – those that are important for your organisation only. Or a few phone calls might give you enough information to get going. Remember: always look for managers' benefits and include them in your answers!

*Tip 19: **Give your managers a helicopter!*** It's often hard to maintain an overview, to see the bigger picture. It helps tremendously when managers have easy access to that bigger picture.

Build a high-quality intranet site for this. You will find all the information you need to do this in the next section.

How to use the intranet to promote your strategy and its execution

More and more companies are using an intranet site as a 'rich' communication channel for a variety of subjects.

And I believe it's a great channel to position and promote your strategy and its execution as well. Here are the benefits:
- You centralise the important information in one place so the information is easily accessible.
- You use the latest technology, which will especially attract your younger and technology-minded managers.
- It forces you to build, and crystallises, the big picture. Since everything is gathered together on the site, it's crucial that everything fits together. This demands an extra effort, but experience teaches us that this is a wonderful tool for eliminating overlaps and reducing complexity.
- You promote Strategy Execution.

 Performance tip. If you don't have the resources for an intranet, you can work with folders on the network as well.

What should you have on your site?

There are no strict rules. Use your creativity. In what follows you will find a list that you can use for inspiration.

- An attractive introduction page.
- The Strategy Execution principles and framework.
- Explain why Strategy Execution is important for your company.
- An overview of the Strategy Execution process and the role of the manager.
- A summary of the strategy and a breakdown per unit.
- Some external information on Strategy Execution.
- A link with reward and talent management.
- The scores on your Strategy Execution Barometer®.
- Best practices organised around different topics.
- How to develop yourself: self-development and promotion development offer.
- Several video interviews including one with the CEO.

Performance tip. An example intro page of a performance management intranet site.

Dear Senior Manager

Welcome to the new performance management site. Whatever brought you here, we hope you find this intranet site interesting, informative, perhaps even inspiring... but above all helpful to make your life as a manager easier.

What will you find here today?

☑ The workshop material from last year's individual objective setting.

☑ Useful guidelines and tips to cascade your strategy.

☑ More on pay for performance at ING.

☑ Insights into the 8, our performance management framework.

☑ Your role within the performance management process.

☑ An outside view of performance management.

☑ Available training and support.

Start browsing through the site – and please do send us your comments.

Erik Dralans
CEO, ING South-West Europe

By now you have an idea what to put on the site. Here are 14 tried and tested tips to get you started with building one or help you boost your existing intranet site.

Tip 1: Start small. It's best to start with a light version and gradually add new material. Focus on the basics. But aim for top quality.

*Tip 2: **Write great copy***. Most business copy is poor quality, often long-winded and overly technical. Make yours different. Use simple language and short sentences. Have a look at the copywriters' section tips for more ideas on how to make your content compelling.

*Tip 3: **Optimise ease-of-use***. Most companies have fixed intranet structures and guidelines that you will need to respect. There are however a few things that make a big difference and can be adopted within almost every structure. Here's a list:
- Limit the number of levels, that is, the number of pages you need to open to access the information.
- Provide different paths to get to the same information.
- Think window shopping. Make your site visually attractive.
- Provide breadcrumbs, ensure that readers know where they are on your site.
- Stick to established web standards like clicking on a logo takes you back to the homepage, links are blue and underlined and clicked links change colour.
- Use persistent navigation (read 'in same place on every page') that includes a way home and a search method.
- Avoid fancy drop-down or fly-out menus; they may look sharp, but are not user-friendly.
- Make sure that the browser's 'back' button actually works on all pages.
- Ensure easy printing by avoiding frames and using an easy print button.

*Tip 4: **Promote your site***. Your site won't be known unless you get the word out. Make sure it's promoted in your other communication channels such as newsletters, team meetings and video. Refer people to your site. Make it the centrepiece of your communication on strategy and its execution.

*Tip 5: **Manage the content***. Once you have your site up-and-running, you need to make sure it is kept up-to-date. Organise a regular clean-up possibly carried out by several people but with one person in charge.

Tip 6: *Provide facts and figures.* People love facts and figures. Satisfy their cravings. Google is the ideal fact collector. You could also have a look at the free performance library on *the performance factory* website: www.the-performance-factory.com/free-performance-library. Do your research.

Tip 7: *Tell great stories.* People also love stories. A boring memo on budgeting becomes a fascinating story when the same content is delivered as an interview with the CFO. Be creative: put your content in a story format and your message will get the attention it deserves.

Tip 8: *Make it easy for people to learn.* Many companies have great development material to help you build your Strategy Execution skills but it's often hidden away in multi-day training manuals. Provide an easy-to-use learning index. This makes it easy for people to track down the information they want. You could also provide a monthly skills highlight.

Tip 9: *Don't develop this channel into a second ERP*. Keeping track of KPIs and individual performance evaluation documents belong somewhere else. Limit yourself to clear information about the strategy, the Strategy Execution steps, and the to-do items for managers.

Tip 10: *Keep your eyes on your target group*. Make sure your messages appeal to your target audience. It often helps to have a sounding board to test ideas, wording, etc. before you go live.

Tip 11: *Don't build a second e-learning platform*. It's great to provide readers with learning opportunities. It's even crucial. Just be careful of the IT impact of the choices you make. You don't want to create an e-learning platform.

Tip 12: *Avoid a collection of documents without the glue.* The overview is crucial. It is the link that ties it altogether. As mentioned in Tip 1, I would suggest starting small and focusing on the glue. You don't want your site to become a document dumping ground.

You should not only evaluate the content but also reflect on the relevance of the content with regards to the overall objective. In other words, see your site as a book on strategy and its execution. Each document needs to fit in somehow and play its mutual part. To avoid producing a cumbersome 500-page book, you need to make decisions regarding which information is the most relevant to your company's specific situation.

*Tip 13: **Make your site attractive***. Satisfy all senses. Make it visually attractive so readers will come back and tell others about it. Make use of modern trends such as videos and blogs.

*Tip 14: **Look beyond your company walls.*** Post best-practices from other companies. Collaborate with universities. Invite experts to add material. You don't need to stop at your company gate.

A view on Strategy Execution by Shane Dempsey, Vice President Human Resources and Communications Europe, Novo Nordisk

What do you consider to be the most important Strategy Execution challenge for an executive team?
I believe an executive team needs to tackle quite a few execution challenges with professionalism and persistence.

The first challenge

The first execution challenge that comes to mind is creating the necessary buy-in for the strategy from the start. An executive team needs to get everyone on board in order to be successful at Strategy Execution. You don't need 100 percent of your organisation enthused about your strategy or ambition – it's not as black and white as this. If you don't have the majority of the organisation behind the overall ambition however, execution becomes a far bigger challenge. To help achieve this, you need driving agents in critical points within the organisation who are aligned with the message.

The second challenge

The second execution challenge for an executive team is to incorporate the human elements in the right way. Senior managers are often great at translating strategy into financials – the profit and loss side of the business – and capturing predictions into budget cycles and rolling forecasts, but tend to forget to build a *sound human strategy*.

More specifically, what are the short-term execution capabilities we need and what are the long-term competences we have to develop as an organisation in order to win the competitive battle? You cannot fire everyone and re-hire every time you adjust your strategy. You need a professional, long-term road map to transform the workforce. A professional workforce plan stabilises your organisation. And the faster the execution needs to happen, the more important the planning side of the human transformation becomes.

Most senior managers will acknowledge what I just said, but few of us truly know how to develop such professional workforce planning, or understand how it needs to fit with the other execution elements. Quite a few executives believe that having a strong human resources division is the answer to the challenge. But having a strong HR partner who is knowledgeable about workforce planning and its crucial role in Strategy Execution, is only part of the solution. The organisation needs a strong planning and development process built on best practices, driven by the managers: its needs to be put in place, nurtured and grown into a specific competence. You may pick up the basis at a business school or even copy it from your next-door neighbour but remember that for each organisation it's unique and therefore, different.

But there are a few things that will help you get the job done. Here are a few tips based on my experience:
- Provide managers with an implementation kit that contains information, skills development material and tools.
- Build workforce planning into your annual budgeting process. This will ensure a closed loop between your strategy, financials and human resources. And, as this is a recurring process involving all managers, it will ensure that the human element in Strategy Execution

isn't forgotten. But remember: make the connection non-intrusive. The processes need to fit together and reinforce each other.

- Don't ever forget the following: workforce planning isn't just about how many people you need, it's about the key competences your organisation needs to develop in order to make strategy happen.
- Don't mix talent management with workforce planning. They are different processes and need to happen in a certain order. Before you start your workforce planning, make sure you have a good view of where the organisation stands in terms of talent. This will instil realism into the workforce planning exercise.
- Discuss people development at every opportunity. Many companies turn it into a 'once-a-year' discussion that results in a nice binder that nobody reads. I'm a strong believer in talent discussions happening regularly. It should be a way of being. It should be a habit – an addiction – to discuss people, talents and development at every opportunity. By doing it this way, your structured workforce planning becomes part of managing. You already know where you stand in terms of competences and people and you don't need to add an additional process or fixed structure. I see it as a key challenge for any organisation to move away from the classical annual talent cycle and evolve towards ongoing discussions about getting the best out of individuals. It's a big step forwards in the execution maturity process.

The third challenge

The third major execution challenge I see for the leadership team is to ensure that everyone has great individual objectives. And in order to get there, most companies have to re-think their objective-setting process completely. Tying objective setting to the strategy for everyone in the organisation is not impossible. Everyone from the chief executive to those on the shop floor should feel they are contributing to success. If you can build it into a solid, ongoing activity which includes regular feedback and coaching, I've experienced that execution results will improve significantly. Of course, an effective review of achievement is easier said than done. Calibrated performance ratings help us to agree on who our best performers really are, not just identifying the people we like the most.

The fourth challenge

The fourth challenge is creating employee engagement through high-quality internal communication. Many companies focus heavily on external communication, but tend to perform poorly on the internal side. And while effective external communication is, and will remain crucial, you don't want your employees reading the newspaper to find out what's going on in their own organisation. Having a strong internal communication strategy as part of your overall execution strategy, is a must.

The fifth challenge

The fifth execution challenge I see is about project work or initiative management. I think we can all agree that strategic initiatives should be staffed with the best possible people, as the success of these projects will determine the organisation's future. Unfortunately, this isn't the general practice. I would summarise the problem as follows. A manager gets a request to provide resources for a project. S/he thinks: 'Is this project really key for the organisation' or 'If I hand over my best resource, I may have trouble reaching my other objectives and that jeopardises my bonus' or 'I cannot reward on success of the project so I will get in trouble with my best employee at the end of the year'. All of these reflections push the manager to avoid the nomination of his best resources.

Strategic initiatives aren't part of daily work and often don't show up in the evaluation at the end of the year. So getting the staffing right for those initiatives is a major challenge for the executive team.

In my experience, to solve the problem, companies should optimise the following four elements:

1. The organisation needs to show all employees the big picture – the link between each project and the future success of the organisation.
2. A company should challenge each new initiative in a pragmatic, consistent way. It's easy to launch new projects that add some value,

but resources are scarce so there needs to be a focus on those projects that bring the most value to the organisation.

3. Employees need to be convinced that the organisation has a solid process in place to weed out the projects that add limited value and leave only the key ones remaining. This is done by open communication and showing consistently that only those projects that make a big difference to the realisation of the strategy come through and others are killed.

4. The final, but maybe most important element, is to implement a solid and fair process to reward and recognise the contribution of individuals to these key projects.

What Strategy Execution advice would you give to an ambitious manager?

There are quite a few I can think of. The four most important ones for me are:

1. *Learn to listen.* Everyone has beliefs, opinions and ideas. As a manager, it's your job to collect all of them and mold them, together with the team, into a shared belief. This only works when you are able to pick up what's going on in the heads of others. And in order to do so, they need to explain their thoughts and you need to capture them and do something with them. It will also require you to step over your ego since it is so much easier to say 'I'm the boss and this is how we are going to do things from today' rather than to listen to others.

2. *Spend some time in a human resources role.* Several successful companies used, and still use, a rotation policy to allow young managers to spend some time in a human resources role to get familiar with people processes such as reward, talent management, objective setting and their inherent complexities. That will build a good foundation later on when you are getting involved in human strategy development.

3. *Work on your basic skill set first.* Start by building your basic management skills such as coaching and communication before you run off to a fancy leadership training course. Build your basic skills

first. You will be grateful that you invested in them at the start of your career as you will need them for the rest of your life.

4. *Coach and be coached.* Coaching is the single most important element for managing a team. Solid coaching skills help you to provide the team, and each individual, with the necessary feedback to boost performance. Unfortunately, many managers don't understand what coaching is all about. You need to invest time and effort to make it your own and develop a style that fits your personality. Make sure you find yourself a coach as well. I'm a big fan of external coaches who can bring an outside perspective into an organisation.

Based on your experience, what is a classic Strategy Execution mistake?

Two immediately come to mind.

The first one is that organisations lose track of their strategy because they are busy dealing with unforeseen regulatory changes, other industry changes, or stock market pressure. And while you cannot ignore them, it's crucial to evaluate the 'real' importance, define actions if needed, and quickly move back to your original focus. You gave your strategy a lot of thought and you cannot be distracted with the 'flavour of the market' to take you away from that focus. It's probably much easier for companies with private ownership, but being stock traded is no excuse to diverge from your strategy because a junior analyst wrote a negative article in last month's trade magazine.

The second one relates to executives' egos. You probably know what I mean: a new manager arrives, finds everything his predecessor did was garbage, throws everything in the bin and starts from zero. A company needs to deal with the egos of newly arrived executives and safeguard those parts of the strategy that work well.

Looking at Strategy Execution from a 'human resources department' point of view, what are important topics for you?

The human resources department should not be seen as the solution to all Strategy Execution people issues. Yes, the HR team can be a big contributor to your overall success, but the people strategy should be owned by all managers and embedded in the way of management. In many cases, HR mistakenly takes over the responsibilities of poor managers just to keep things moving.

As we upgrade the role of the HR business partner, we need to commit to coaching for success and stop sweeping the weaknesses of our management partners under the carpet. This means broader business understanding and, most importantly, passion. Successful HR business partnering relies on the business coming first. If you're not passionate about the business, passion for HR will only take you so far.

PERFORMANCE TAKEAWAYS

- Communication about the strategy and its execution comes in varying shapes and forms. It ranges from individual conversations during objective setting over group interactions around the Balanced Scorecard, intranet postings to writing a memo for the whole organisation regarding a strategy shift.
- Great communication helps you to get the strategy into the *heads, hearts* and *hands* of the people. It creates *understanding, motivation* and *action*.
- Communication is a crucial management skill. Make it your ambition to play in the premier league.
- New technologies create new communication opportunities. Build a great intranet site and promote your strategy and its execution.

And the answer is? 'Communicate: 121, 1210 and 12100 or more'.
Communication comes in different shapes and forms. That's what the title is referring to. You communicate to another individual (121), a team (1210), a department (12100), or...

But no matter what the shape and form, the quality of your communication will have an impact – either positive or negative – on your Strategy Execution quality.

So make it your mission to be the best communicator you can be in all types of situations. Work on your communication skills. You are never too old or too good to learn.

Communicate like a pro and get your strategy in the heads, hearts and hands of your people!
- Heads: You want everyone to understand the strategy.
- Hearts: You want everyone to be motivated by the strategy.
- Hands: You want everyone to take action to get things done.

CHAPTER V

Challenge 3: Coach: Become a 3% member

"The best time to make up your mind about people is never"
– Katharine Hepburn in *The Philadelphia Story*

In 1999, a tall man walks into a room packed with people. He asks 'Who wants to be coached?'. Many glance surprisedly at each other. This isn't what they had expected.

After a few seconds of complete silence, people respond by raising their hands. Then the tall man starts asking a series of questions for each person to answer in silence on paper.

The session took 40 minutes and, at the end, more than 75 percent of the people in the room answered 'yes' to the question 'Have you been coached?'.

I was in the room that day and… one of that 75 percent. From that moment on, I became a coaching adept. Our coach, the tall man, was David Hemery, John's colleague and the 1968 Olympics 400-metre hurdles gold medallist. If you aren't a coaching fan yet, I hope you will be after reading this chapter.

Strategy Execution is made up of many, MANY individual execution efforts – an infinite to-do list taken up by different people at different times.

Performance coaching helps this process by creating the necessary commitment with the individuals involved to move these actions forwards. In other words, coaching creates engagement to get things done.

This chapter provides a clear overview of the key elements of coaching and gives proven tips to upgrade your coaching skills. It will also provide you with ideas on how coaching can benefit the organisation.

What every performance-oriented manager should know about coaching

- Coaching is a relatively new field. Although Socrates launched some of the basic principles of modern coaching some 2000 years ago, it has only become well-known over the last two decades.
- In these last 20 years, coaching has had a meteoric rise in popularity. Eighty percent of UK organisations are investing in one or more forms of coaching and the International Coaching Federation is attracting record numbers each month.
- To this day, there is no single agreed upon definition for coaching. Some are straightforward, others are fancy.
- My favourite coaching definition is by Tim Gallwey, John's former business partner and author of several best-selling books on coaching in sport. It goes like this: *"Coaching is unlocking a person's potential to maximise their own performance. It's helping them to learn rather than teaching them"*.
- Be careful not to mix performance coaching with counselling. Coaching is work-related, proactive and focused on conscious or just below the surface things. Counselling is a whole different ball game. It's non-work-related, rather reactive and concerned with the core beliefs of an individual. You can do more harm than good by mixing them up.

    In his article *The Very Real Dangers of Executive Coaching* (*Harvard Business Review*), Steve Berglas pinpoints the risks – and unfortunately – the practice of unschooled coaches who enter into more psychotherapy issues with their coachee than they can competently handle.

    Make sure you do not make the same mistake. If you suspect a work-related issue has deeper origins, call in a professional with the necessary skills. If you are on the receiving end, make sure you have a profile that fits your needs.

- Coaching is all about unlocking future potential performance rather than evaluating and judging current performance. It's based on the belief that individuals want to and can do a good job. If, deep down, you don't believe this, coaching is probably not for you.

- Performance coaching is not so much about passing on individual performance objectives, but rather a technique to take away the barriers that prevent individuals from actually taking on and delivering against these objectives.

- Coaching is also a way of managing rather than a tool to use in a variety of situations such as planning, delegation or problem solving. It's a different way of viewing people – a far more optimistic way than most of us are accustomed to – and results in a different way of treating them.

- There are many coaching methods. The good ones will help you as a coach to facilitate learning rather than to direct it. Questioning techniques and active listening are your primary means to do this.

- Everybody can become a coach. It's a skill that requires only time and effort to develop. It's probably harder to give up instructing than it is to learn to coach.

- Most companies today invest in coaching to improve individual performance. But more and more companies realise there is so much more to gain if they can harvest the individual benefits to improve the overall company performance.

- There is no single ideal way of measuring the coaching ROI for companies – although many claim to have the best.

Grow Me: Coaching individuals with the best-known coaching model in the world

There are dozens of coaching methods out there, some better than others. The good ones will help you as a coach to facilitate learning rather than to direct it.

GROW – originally conceived by Graham Alexander and further perfected by John – is probably the best-known and appreciated coaching technique in the world.

The GROW model
G – Goal setting
R – Reality
O – Options
W – Will

Unlike other techniques, it is much more than a toolbox linked to an acronym. It's an approach, a philosophy which helps you create the right context to help individuals transform their potential into peak performance. And I believe that's exactly the reason for its success.

It's my objective here to outline the main points. If you would like to know more, you should get yourself a copy of John's book *Coaching for Performance*.

The essence of good coaching: create awareness and build responsibility with the performer

You can achieve limited success by diligently following the GROW road map explained in the book. But without subscribing to the underlying coaching philosophy however, you will fall short of what is truly possible.

The essence of good coaching is all about you, as a coach, helping your coachee to increase awareness and take responsibility. Of course, the process is important since it brings structure to the conversation, but it should not be the cornerstone of your coaching. Creating awareness and responsibility are.

Frame your coaching in the context of awareness and responsibility and it will improve drastically.

Awareness: collecting high-quality relevant input

Our minds can only process a limited amount of information at the same time. We have a mechanism in our brain that filters all incoming signals and only those considered important come through. It would be impossible to function without it.

This selection process takes place automatically without any conscious effort. You don't have to do anything. You can however feed your brain better input and influence the importance given to certain inputs.

By being aware – or in other words by tuning your senses and engaging your brain – you are in control of the quality of input that your brain receives and the importance it is given.

So how does this relate to coaching?

Performance coaching aims to increase performance – the output. The output increases when there's better input. And you improve input through awareness.

So if you can help your coachee to increase awareness and thereby help to collect better input, you dramatically increase the possibility of increased output. (I will talk about responsibility – the other crucial element needed for success – in the next section).

As a coach, you cannot tell someone to become aware. It's up to the coachee to direct and engage his brain through focus. By asking the right questions however, you can facilitate this process.

Let's do a little exercise on input quality and awareness to make it more concrete. I will be your coach.

Here is your assignment. I would like you to have an animated, mutually interesting discussion with someone about coaching and Strategy Execution within the next three days.

To do this, you will need to identify the person and have a conversation about the coaching. The better you manage the input – in this case the choice of the individual and the content preparation – the more chance you will have of reaching the objective – that is, having a mutually interesting discussion with someone about coaching and Strategy Execution in the next three days.

I could tell you to select the best possible candidate or to read this chapter twice in order to get a good grasp of what coaching is all about… but I will not raise your input quality and therefore will have no impact on your success.

In order to help you, I need to increase your awareness.

Let's see if I can do that by asking you some questions. It would be great if you could write the answers down.

- Who would be the five people that could be interested in knowing more about coaching?
- On what page do you find information about coaching that gets you excited?
- What would be the best way to also get one or more of the five people you identified excited?
- How do you find out what they would like to learn about coaching?
- What other chapters could help you prepare?
- In what way can you use this book to get the conversation about coaching started?

These questions make you think and automatically engage you in the exercise. If you have taken the time to reflect on each question, you should have a much better idea as to who to talk to (one crucial input element) as well as some ideas on what you want to talk about (the other crucial input element).

So by asking you these questions, I have hopefully enabled you to raise your awareness and facilitated the collection of better quality input for the assignment.

One final remark: besides awareness, there's also self-awareness. If awareness is 'knowing what is happening around you', self-awareness is 'knowing what you are experiencing at this moment'. It's another brain and body process that you have at your disposal to collect valuable input.

 Performance tip. You might also want to explore self-coaching. Sport activities are a great place to start. If you are into tennis, skiing or golf, you could get yourself one of the series of Tim Gallwey books, *The Inner Game of...*

It's great and fun to read.

I've improved my skiing tremendously and picked up new angles on coaching at the same time.

So what are you experiencing at the moment? Still thinking about the exercise? Enthusiastic to have those discussions? Hungry (one has to eat)? Curious to read on?

This auto-feedback – available for you at all times – helps you take better decisions.

So take a moment to evaluate the input signals from your brain and body, read on, continue to work on your assignment... or grab something to eat!

Responsibility: the performer's choice to take ownership

Responsibility is the second important performance coaching concept. When you truly accept responsibility for your thoughts and actions, you will raise your commitment to them. And this inevitably leads to better performance.

Your performance will not improve when you are ordered or expected to be responsible – or even if you are given responsibility. You might do the job to avoid an implied threat or punishment but your performance is unlikely to be optimised.

So what do you require to create responsibility?

You need to have a choice. And with choice comes responsibility.

Let's return to your assignment. Imagine for one moment that the person you talk to doesn't react as enthusiastically as you had hoped. Who will you blame?

Me probably, as I asked you to take action. This illustrates where you currently see the responsibility lying. As long as you blame someone else, there is no real sense of ownership.

As a coach, by asking questions, I can help you with the reflection process but the final decision is up to you. It always is, even if that choice is to take no action.

So, to conclude, merely telling someone to be responsible for something does not make them feel responsible. That comes with choice. Offering choice is a fantastic trigger for responsibility.

So, it's up to you. Please decide if, and how, you want to take the assignment further. And if you choose to do so, please let me know the result. I would appreciate the feedback.

Ask the right questions, in the right order and… listen to the responses

You know now that the best way to develop and maintain the ideal state of mind for performance is to build awareness and responsibility. They are the two key elements that your coaching should focus on.

Asking questions – rather than telling – is the best way to mentally engage your coachee. And as you are looking for the highest possible engagement from your coachee, asking questions therefore becomes your most important means of communication.

'But what questions do I ask?' might be the next question on your mind.

Well, your questions need to evoke awareness and responsibility with your coachee. Random questioning will not work.

Effective questioning can be broken down into two parts: asking the *right questions* and asking them in the *right order*. For the former, have a look at tips in the next section. Several of them will help you to ask the right questions. I will explain the questioning order below.

 Performance download 11. High-quality coaching questions – examples.

But before I move on to the sequencing framework for questioning, let me point out one other crucial point.

Interact!

Yes, that's it. Interact. Coaching is like dancing the salsa: one person leads but the dance evolves due to the interaction between the two dancers. This makes each dance unique, even if you always dance with the same partner.

Coaching is the same. Each coaching session, whether formal or informal, is unique, even if the coachee is the same. It's all about human interaction.

So, as a coach, you should be leading the overall conversation while expecting interaction. A good coach will follow the coachee's chain of thought while also monitoring how that relates to the overall subject and coaching process.

A good coach switches off the autopilot. Be flexible and respond to the coachee's verbal and non-verbal communication of the coachee. The better you are engaged, the easier it is to react.

One way to engage yourself further is to listen to yourself. Not in a bizarre way, but by being self-aware.

In the back of your mind, ask yourself these questions: 'How am I reacting?', 'Am I judging?', 'Am I leaning forwards or backwards?' or 'Am I trying to find a solution myself?'. This questioning will keep your mind on the game and increase your awareness. It demands, as with all skills, some practice to do everything simultaneously. But in the end, it will make you a far better coach.

A sequencing framework for your questions – GROW

The GROW coaching model offers the coach a simple, yet powerful, framework. It helps you to structure your interaction with your coachee.

When the coaching is formal, always start with the first stage, even when you cannot precisely define the goal. You can always return to the first stage when both of you have gained more insight from the other stages.

When the coaching is informal, it's usually a good idea to initially follow the coachee's lead by asking a few questions to trigger more detail, than move into the sequence.

The conversation can start at any one of the four stages of the GROW model. A coachee might begin by telling you about something s/he wants to achieve (Goal), a current problem (Reality), a new idea for improving things (Options) or by outlining an action plan (Will).

By itself, the particular order of questions will not help you to become a great coach. Each question should aim to increase your coachee's awareness and responsibility. It's the combination of context and sequence, along with lots of practice, that will make you a better coach.

G for Goal setting: define the short- and long-term goals

The most important part of the first coaching phase is to define and agree upon one or more goals that the coachee wishes to achieve. Ideally, you should establish a clear goal for the coaching session itself *and* a long-term performance goal.

Make sure that you and your coachee know what the objective of your conversation is, even when you are coaching informally. It's important to give value and direction to any discussion.

There's a whole chapter on individual objective setting, as it is not only a crucial stage for performance coaching but for Strategy Execution in general. Goal setting is one of the most researched elements in organisational science. I believe every good coach needs a solid understanding of the topic that goes beyond knowing what SMART stands for. For more information, see Chapter 3.

R for Reality: explore the current situation

The most important criterion for examining the current situation is objectivity. Most people think they are objective but in reality they are not. Nobody is. Absolute objectivity doesn't exist. We can only have partial objectivity.

There are many things that can and will cloud your, and your coachee's objectivity including opinions, expectations, fear and prejudices. But the more we aim to be objective, the more we will be.

So it's your challenge to come as close as possible to reality, by-passing as many distortions as possible. As a coach, you should help your coachee to remove as many false assumptions as possible.

Explore the real nature of the problem by asking your coachee to describe their perceived current reality. This is an important step. Too often, people try to solve a problem without fully considering their starting point – and often they are missing some of the information they need to solve the problem effectively. All too often, as your coachee tells you about his current Reality, the solution starts to emerge.

O for Options: identify and evaluate different action strategies

Once you and your coachee have explored the current reality, it's time to explore what is possible – meaning all the potential options, behaviour or decisions that could lead to the right solution.

Help your coachee to generate a long list. Your objective as a coach during the Options stage should not be to find the right answer, but to help your coachee identify as many different ideas and solutions as possible. You don't want any obstacles like preferences, feasibility or need for completeness blocking the brainstorming process. At this point in the process, it's the ideation – the creative part – that provides the real value.

So, as strange as it may seem, focus on quantity rather than quality and feasibility. It's from this long inventory of creative possibilities that actions will be chosen during the next stage.

W for Will: what will you do by when?
The purpose of this final phase is to transform a discussion into a decision, using the outcomes of the three previous coaching steps. Again, you will be guiding your coachee through a series of questions.

By examining the current Reality and exploring the Options, your coachee will now have a good idea of how s/he can achieve their goal. That's great, but without ownership to kick-start and drive future actions, it has no value. So you need to help your coachee to take responsibility and commit to action. As you want to maximise chances for success, you need to examine any potential obstacles, discuss ways of overcoming them, agree on the resources needed and the nature of further support.

So, the fourth phase demands that the coachee takes several decisions. Remember: the coachee takes the decision, even if that decision is to take no action at all. The coachee always maintains choice and ownership.

Thirty tips to become a better performance coach

Now that you have learnt the art of questioning within the context of awareness and responsibility, here are some practical coaching tips to boost your coaching.

There is no one way of coaching all individuals in all situations. The list below is therefore incomplete and even has some contradictory tips. But they have all been tested and will be useful for you as a coach somewhere along your growth path.

You might want to read a section at a time, highlighting or taking notes as you go through them.

As your coaching evolves, so will your needs for further development. It might therefore be a good idea to run through this list every few months. You will see that, after some time, certain tips will hold no mystery for you anymore and others will attract your attention and reveal different nuances over time.

> **Performance download 12.** Select the right coaching tips – a checklist.

1. *Ask open questions*. Asking closed questions (read 'questions with yes/no answer') prevents people from thinking. Asking open questions causes them to think for themselves.

2. *Make your coachee think.* Ask open questions that demand your coachee to focus more than usual to give accurate answers.

   Here's an example: 'Can you summarise in three headlines the added value of awareness and responsibility for your coaching activities in the future?' rather than 'What do you remember from the previous chapter?'.

3. *Don't be judgemental*. Ask open questions that demand descriptive, non-judgemental answers. This way, you avoid causing self-criticism or damaging your coachee's self-esteem.

4. *Resist the Why? question*. Asking why often implies criticism and triggers the coachee's analytical thinking process. And analysis (thinking) and awareness (observing) are two different mental processes that are virtually impossible to combine to full effect.

   So aim for questions that start with words such as what, when, who, how much and how many.

5. *Keep it short*. Make your coaching questions clear and unambiguous. It helps when you limit yourself to one brief question. And listen for the response before launching a new question.

6. *Go on a trip*. A useful metaphor for the GROW model is the plan you might make for an important journey. First, you start with a map

that helps your coachee decide where they are going (their Goal) and establish where they currently are (their current Reality). Then you explore various ways (the Options) of making the journey. In the final step, establishing the Will, you ensure your coachee is committed to making the journey.

7. *Go undercover*. You don't need a formal coaching session to raise someone's awareness and responsibility. In fact, most coaching takes place unsolicited, with the coachee unaware of the process. The coached individual will simply think that you were being particularly helpful and considerate. This means that every conversation you have becomes a potential testing ground – a learning experience – to improve your coaching skills.

8. *Ask for, and be open to feedback*. Everybody learns, even the best coaches. So do ask for feedback from your coachee. Besides the positive learning experience for you, it has the extra benefit for improving the relationship. You increase the chances that your coachee will be more open to feedback when s/he is next on the receiving end as feedback is becoming part of the way you interact.

9. *Set goals at the start with a self-evaluation form*. I have mentioned before how important it is to begin the coaching process, formal or informal, with a clear definition of what your coachee would like to achieve. Using a self-evaluation form helps this process tremendously. There are many lists on the internet, or if you can't find one that suits your needs, build one. With as few as 10 questions you can offer your coachee your first added value.

10. *Don't let the good guys get away*. When coaching for performance, you aim to improve certain performance shortcomings of your coachee. But remember, it's not all bad all of the time. I'm sure you can find several good, even great, behaviours that your coachee possesses.

But without the proper attention, s/he might not be aware of them, or even worse, adds them to the list of behaviours that need to change.

Make sure you identify those positive behaviours and help your coachee leverage them. It's a great way to stress the positive *and* help your coachee reach goals faster by building on existing strengths at the same time.

11. ***Coach only on first-hand data***. When you know the coachee, you probably have more information available. You might, for example, have heard something from a colleague.

   And I know it's tempting to use that information, but be aware that using it will often have a negative impact on your coaching relationship – whether the information is correct or not.

   So stick to what you hear directly from your coachee.

12. ***Dig deeper***. Ask your coachee open questions that will make him reflect. You should be able to detect it from their body language such as a pause before answering or a raising of the eyes.

   When you ask questions solely from the normal, conscious level of awareness, you may be helping your coachee to structure his thoughts but you are not probing for deeper levels of awareness.

   But when your coachee has to really dig deep to find the answer, new awareness is created. And once found, the input becomes conscious and readily available for the coachee to use.

13. ***Coach or tell?*** Whether or not to opt for a coaching approach depends on your situation at a given moment. If timing is the most important criterion in a specific situation, such as in a crisis, doing the job yourself or telling someone exactly what to do is probably your best option. If quality matters most, you will get the best results with coaching for high awareness and responsibility. If learning and retention are crucial, coaching is again your best choice.

14. ***Before you start, ask yourself what you want to get out of it***. Don't confuse or fool yourself by pretending to coach when you are actually doing something different. If you want to teach, then go and teach. If you want to sell, then do so. But don't use coaching as a

means to something other than for what it is intended. It might give you the desired outcome in the short-term but will always backfire and create more problems at a later stage.

15. **Understand what makes people tick**. There is no need to complete a psychology degree before you can start coaching. But as coaching is all about human interaction, it's useful to have a basic understanding of what drives human behaviour.

16. **Use homework**. It gives your coachee more time to collect high-quality input and creates responsibility. And it will give you more coaching time and a solid starting base for your next session.

17. **Delegate coaching**. Evaluate carefully the amount of time you allocate to coaching. In some situations you can delegate particular coaching jobs to others.

18. **Coach the coach**. When delegating a coaching job to someone else, you are stimulating that individual to apply and build their own coaching skills. It further enriches your own coaching practice as you are approaching coaching from a new perspective.

    Even after years of coaching, I still find it refreshing and rewarding to coach coaches.

19. **Don't feel guilty about providing input**. Just because you read somewhere that a coach should not delve into the content, doesn't mean that you can't provide some input. You just need to be careful with your timing and delivery method.

    A good time to offer your knowledge or experience is when you recognise that the coachee has exhausted all possibilities during the Option phase – the 'O' from GROW.

    Ask the following question: 'I have some more options and ideas. Maybe you would like to hear them?' You can style the question to your liking, but do make sure that it's clear to your coachee that you are momentarily stepping out of your facilitating role.

    When providing your input, make it as short as possible. Try to put it all into one phrase. You don't want to be talking for the next 10 minutes.

If you have more then one session and know the topic, you can write your tips on paper and get a feeling for the tone and directness of the message.

Remember to make it clear to your coachee that your input should be treated in the same way as his/her own options and ideas.

20. **When you don't know the answer, admit it.** A no-nonsense approach will help your build a relationship of trust. It is extremely damaging to that relationship to go back on something that you supported during a previous session. If you don't have the answer, say so and offer to find it by the next session or possibly earlier.

21. **Two might be better than one.** You may find it easier to coach two people at the same time. It might sound strange as, like most people, you probably have the image of coaching as a strictly one-to-one process. But it's rewarding to look beyond that preconception.

I found that coaching two people at the same time can reduce tension and provide a great opportunity for role-playing.

22. **Describe versus evaluate.** You should use, and encourage your coachee to use descriptive, rather than evaluative words. The more specific and descriptive words and phrases become, the less criticism they tend to carry, and the more productive the coaching will be.

So don't just tell a speaker his presentation was poor or inadequate – this will only make him feel bad. He wants to know that the presentation was clearly structured, brief but rather monotonous and pitched at too low a level for the audience.

Remember that description adds value, criticism detracts.

23. **Coach your boss.** You probably won't get very far by telling your boss what to do. But applying some of the coaching principles and coaching upwards can increase your success rate dramatically.

24. *Go back and forth.* The GROW methodology helps you structure your coaching conversation. It gives a proven, logical sequence to your questions.

But even though there is a sequence, you need to go back and forth between the different steps.

You might start with a vague Goal that only becomes clear after examining the Reality in some detail. It will then be necessary to go back and define the Goal more precisely before moving to the Options. Even a clearly defined Goal might prove itself wrong or inappropriate once the Reality is clear.

Similarly, when listing the Options, it's important to check back if they help to move towards the desired Goal or not.

And finally, before the Will is finalised, it's crucial to see if the action plan, once realised, achieves the Goal.

25. *Don't over prepare*. Too much preparation destroys your flexibility. Develop a general road map for your next session rather than a detailed, step-by-step instruction manual.

26. *Build your communication skills.* These are crucial. Coaching is all about human interaction. Make sure you master a basic communication model. It's better to have a thorough understanding of one model that you can actually apply in practice rather than have only a theoretical background on a few of them. Chapter 4 can help.

27. *Don't strive to put everything into a single session*. If your coachee is motivated for the next session, it's often a first sign that something positive has been put in motion.

28. *Just do it.* Often your coachee will say something like 'When I started the presentation I gave a short introduction. Then it all blocked'.

Instead of talking about something, I often find it useful to ask the coachee to replay a certain situation. It makes it more concrete and offers a great opportunity to test out some of the Options.

When your coachee is able to do a successful role play exercise, the motivation, self-belief and learning curve receive a huge boost.

29. *Provide quick and easy feedback*. Here's a simple but effective feedback method you can use all the time. It's called LCS – which stands for Like, Concern, Suggestion.

Start by saying something you liked, then add your concern and end with one or more suggestions. Here's an example: 'I'm happy you have almost finished reading all these tips. But by only reading them, I'm concerned it will not boost your coaching skills as it is more important to actually put them into practice. So I would suggest picking your three favourite ones and thinking about how you could use them in the assignment I gave you earlier'.

30. *Everything your coachee says is important.* It's your job to find out how it is important.

Grow Us: Coaching from a company perspective

What would happen if all managers in your organisation integrated coaching in their day-to-day behaviour in a consistent and qualitative way?

The benefits would be enormous, wouldn't you agree?

But you'll probably also agree that, while the benefits would be enormous, the road to get there might be quite long and prove to be a real challenge. Even though coaching has seen a great boost, it is still very much seen *and* used as an individual development intervention.

Let's be very clear. Coaching on an individual basis offers many benefits but there's a next step your organisation can take. And this step can really boost your Strategy Execution. But to reap those benefits, coaching needs to evolve from individual performance coaching to collective performance coaching.

You achieve this by introducing the coaching principles into the management style of all managers. In other words, coaching as your organisation's predominant management style. The 'manager as a coach' who helps colleagues remove individual barriers to facilitate strategy implementation.

In the next section, you will discover five actions that will help your organisation transform into a coaching company.

Five actions to take coaching to the next level in your organisation

Here are five interventions that you as a manager can take to help your organisation take coaching to the next level.

Action 1: Develop and communicate a shared vision on coaching

As I have said before, there is no single, agreed upon, clear coaching definition. When you look closely at what people in your organisation mean by the word 'coaching', you will surely find a wide variety of definitions and approaches.

Take some time to collect these different ideas, definitions and models that exist in your organisation. Select the one you consider to fit best with your organisation or merge the best ones.

Remember to keep it simple and focused on what's important – the context of responsibility and awareness.

Once you have an agreement on the overall coaching framework and definition, your next challenge is to communicate it. You can pick up some tips and advice from Chapter 4.

Action 2: Create a coaching culture

The old 'carrot and stick' management style is past its prime. More and more companies realise people perform better when they take on responsibility because they want to and not because they have to.

It's a growth path for each individual, and the company as a whole, to move from hierarchy to self-responsibility – from a one-way street to a two-way communication highway.

This transition doesn't happen overnight.

In their book *Coaching, Mentoring and Organisational Consultancy*, Peter Hawkins and Nick Smith describe the seven different stages in the evolution of a coaching culture. They can help you identify where your company is at today and give you an idea on the next steps to aim for.

Here they are:

- *Stage 1*. The organisation employs coaches for some of its executives.
- *Stage 2*. The organisation develops its own coaching and mentoring capacity.
- *Stage 3*. The organisation actively supports coaching endeavours.
- *Stage 4*. Coaching is a norm for individuals, teams and the whole organisation.
- *Stage 5*. Coaching is embedded in the HR and performance management processes of the organisation.
- *Stage 6*. Coaching is the predominant style of managing throughout the organisation.
- *Stage 7*. Coaching is 'how we do business' with all our stakeholders.

Action 3: Understand and solve the drama triangle

Coaching is, in most cases, a conversation between two people, a one-on-one human interaction. But the benefits shouldn't be limited to those two people in the room. Coaching should add value for the organisation as well.

This creates the need for a three-way partnership between the organisation, the coachee and the coach. This desired partnership is often called the drama triangle – with the coachee being identified as the victim, the organisation as the persecutor and the coach as the rescuer – as it provides a major challenge to get to a win-win situation.

Be aware of this challenge and discuss it with your colleagues. There are several actions you can take to solve or reduce these tensions. Here are some of them:

- Make sure coaching is not just a nice to have for some key executives but rather a cornerstone of your development approach.
- Organise regular joint meetings with internal and external coaches.
- Focus coaching expenditure on those areas where it can make an organisational difference.

- Develop metrics to measure the coaching added value for the organisation.

Action 4: Implement a coaching development platform

Coaching is a skill that anyone can learn. It just requires time, effort and some persistence. If your organisation is serious about coaching, it's a good idea to have a structured development approach – a coaching development platform. Have a look at Chapter 7 for a detailed explanation.

Action 5: Coach the coach

If you want people to learn and apply coaching, use a coaching approach. I have found that being coached to learn coaching is a great way to progress quickly.

And once you reach a certain maturity, coaching others on coaching gives your learning curve yet another great boost.

It might be helpful to have a coach-the-coach programme institutionalised in your organisation.

A view on Strategy Execution by Douglas Johnson-Poensgen, Vice President Business Development, BT

What do you consider to be the most important Strategy Execution challenge for an executive team?

I believe a top team has quite a few crucial execution challenges. Here's my list:

- *Change the shape of the boat.* When you choose a new strategy, you need to change the way you work. Or in other words, a new strategy demands, in most cases, a different operating model. The boat that got you to your current destination most probably won't get you to the next one. This means that the challenge for an executive is not only to think about the next destination and the journey ahead, but also to make sure that the boat is capable of making the desired trip.

- *Don't rock the boat too much.* Changing an organisation demands a thoughtful approach. It requires a careful balance between enough movement to get things moving forwards and too much movement to make the boat tip over and sink. It's the job of the executive team to trim the boat (read 'organisation') in such a way that the speed is there, but not enough to tip it over. And this demands a great deal of execution experience, a thorough knowledge of the organisation and a solid execution plan.

- *Make clear choices.* A diversified business can increase stability of income. While some businesses get into trouble in certain market conditions, others thrive. The levelling between generates cash flow stability. But a diversified business tremendously increases the execution complexity. The 'one size fits all' approach doesn't apply anymore. Just think about the IT challenges and I'm sure you will know what I mean.

  So, while at first sight, from a strategic perspective, diversification seems a simple choice, taking the execution challenges into consideration makes it much more difficult. So when executives think about a new strategic direction, they need to take into account the execution challenges that create choice. This needs to happen right at the start.

- *Engage your people.* Engagement doesn't come by itself. It demands hard work. And I believe an executive team has two focus areas to create that important employee engagement. The first thing the executive team needs to focus on is translating the complex strategy into an easy story: one that is simple and compelling and captures the essence of the new direction of the organisation.

  Secondly, the story needs to come to life. And this only works through visible leadership. Leaders should be in the front row, set the example and invest lots of time involving the rest of the organisation.

- *Kill perverse incentive systems.* In order to implement your strategy, you want your people to behave in a certain way. It's crucial that your incentive systems reinforce the good behaviour and punish the bad ones, and not vice versa. Let me give you an example. If you want to excel in customer service, you don't want to reward your sales people on revenues alone, as they will be tempted to undersell and accept whatever the customer wants. Easy acceptance by the sales team creates delivery problems at a later stage. By rewarding the sales team based on gross margin results, they will be less tempted to undersell and motivated to involve the delivery team to check if the solution requested is actually feasible. Bring realism into the sales process.

- *Avoid complex financial transfer mechanisms.* There are quite a few organisations that have their own currency, just like in Monopoly. But unlike the game, the complex financial transfer mechanisms demand an army of accountants to track the internal financial streams.

  And while these financial streams can have a positive impact on the sense of ownership, transfer mechanisms are often a heavy burden for the organisation. The issues – extra work and turf wars – quickly outweigh the benefits. I would advise on keeping the internal trading to a minimum, especially below the business unit level.

What Strategy Execution advice would you give to an ambitious manager?

1. *Don't ever forget the customer.* Your company exists thanks to your customers. Make sure you keep them at the centre of all your actions.

2. *Get external input.* The world doesn't stop at your company door. Make sure you keep a broad scope by finding out what other companies are doing, collecting best practices, following industry leaders' current thinking and reading books.

3. *Make a difference.* Be like FedEx: 'No matter how hard the challenge, we make sure we deliver'. Become known as a manager who makes things happen and delivers against his/her promises. Start building your execution reputation early in your career. Too many managers lose precious time working on their 'talking' skills but forget the delivery part. While this might work in the short run, it's deadly in the long-term.

4. *Value people who make a difference.* This builds on the previous tip. While being focused on high-quality delivery, learn to identify others with the same skills and focus. Build a network of people who get things done. Try to get those profiles into your team and make sure you reward them appropriately.

5. *Build thinking and action skills.* Don't stick to one silo on your way to the top. Make sure you regularly shift between 'strategy'-oriented jobs – like strategic planner and 'execution'-driven functions – such as sales or operations. You will never gain those valuable 'crossover' insights if you stick to one lane.

6. *Practice visible leadership.* Visible leadership is key to creating engagement to move things forwards. For some, it comes naturally but most of us have to learn it on the job. Start your practice early and refine it along the way. It's a great skill that will serve you well throughout your career but especially when you reach the senior level in the organisation.

7. *Always remember the 1/3 rule.* This might be my most important advice. Let me explain my point with an example. Imagine you have one year to turn a business around. You don't want to spend more than 33 percent of your time on the strategy and planning phase. So without any further planning, you know when you should start the execution phase. This approach ensures that there is enough time available for executing the great ideas and avoids analysis paralysis.

Based on your experience, what's a classic Strategy Execution mistake?

The biggest execution problem is actually a strategy problem. Great execution can only be built on a great strategy. Without a great strategy, there will be never a great execution. You need to make certain that the starting point is okay. This requires making quite a few tough choices. One typical error is to get going without having made these crucial decisions in the hope that they will get clearer down the road during implementation. But they never do. And by that point, it will be too late.

Looking at Strategy Execution from a 'business development' point of view, what is the most important topic for you?

I would call the most important topic 'free the entrepreneur'. And I believe it's a crucial one for everyone in the organisation, not only business development.

I learnt in the army that no plan survives contact with the enemy. This means that you can spend all the time and money in the world on planning as changes will always be necessary. But the key point is that when certain parts of the plan don't work as intended, it's up to the people in the field to look for alternatives in order to win.

Organisations spend much time and money on making the best possible plans. And you know upfront that not everything will go according to plan. But you do want your employees to take on the execution responsibility, to take ownership for delivering the strategy. And when something doesn't go as planned, to look for alternatives in order to get the job done.

It's important to define clear flexibility guidelines – you don't want everyone running around in all directions, but within these guidelines you need employees to focus on the overall intent and think like entrepreneurs.

PERFORMANCE TAKEAWAYS

– Coaching is a great skill to boost Strategy Execution. It helps remove performance barriers and creates action engagement to take the strategy forwards.

– Coaching is a skill, a technique, that everyone can learn with practice and persistence. There's only five percent theory, the other 95 percent is practice.

– Your main objective is to raise your coachee's awareness and responsibility.

– Questioning is your main instrument to achieve the above.

– The order in which you pose your questions is important. The GROW model helps you to get the sequence right.

– The GROW coaching model offers the coach a simple, yet powerful, framework. It helps you to structure your interaction with your coachee.

  ▪ G for Goal setting: define the short- and long-term goals.

  ▪ R for Reality: explore the current situation.

  ▪ O for Options: identify and evaluate different action strategies.

  ▪ W for Will: what will you do by when?

– Ask the right questions, in the right order and... listen to the responses.

– Coaching is also a way of managing.

– There is no one way of coaching all individuals in all situations.

– To get the most out of coaching for your organisation, you need to work on moving from individual performance coaching to collective performance coaching. Focus on the following five actions:

  ▪ Action 1: Develop and communicate a shared vision on coaching.

  ▪ Action 2: Create a coaching culture.

  ▪ Action 3: Understand and solve the drama triangle.

  ▪ Action 4: Implement a coaching development platform.

  ▪ Action 5: Coach the coach.

– If there is one point you should remember, it's to ask the right questions to raise awareness and responsibility.

And the answer is? 'Coach: Become a 3% member'.

A few years ago, I participated in a large research project. One of the most notable conclusions was that managers believed themselves to be poor coaches. Only three percent believed themselves to be excellent. The result was quite striking, not only because of the low number, but because the same group of managers was far more positive about other skills such as decision taking and strategy development.

PART 3

ORGANISE THE 8

CHAPTER VI

Challenge 4: Simplify: From 100-to-1 in less than 3 years

"Any intelligent fool can make things bigger and more complex. It takes a touch of genius – and a lot of courage – to move in the opposite direction"
– Albert Einstein

"The ability to simplify means to eliminate the unnecessary so that the necessary may speak"
– Hans Hoffmann
Introduction to the Bootstrap

"Simplicity is the ultimate sophistication"
– Leonardo Da Vinci

Japan, 17th century. The old Tokaido, a coastal road connecting the capital Edo – nowadays better known as Tokyo – and the old imperial residence town of Kyoto. Stretching 303 miles (488 kilometres), the Tokaido was the life artery of Japan for trade and protection, some even claiming that the road was fundamental to Japan's success in that era.

The world evolved and so did the route. It became one of the most heavily travelled transportation corridors in the world, mainly due to the construction of the Tokaido Shinkansen railroad, which follows the route and carried the world's first high-speed train service.

The Strategy Execution process is your highway to performance. To be more precise, you should picture your Strategy Execution process not as a single street, but as a network of unique roads – smaller and larger ones – all interlinked together. And your roads carry names like 'strategy review process', 'initiative management process', 'coaching process', 'individual objective-setting process' and so on.

This chapter will help you better understand your unique Strategy Execution process, evaluate its quality and select the right initiatives to continuously improve your execution process into a rock-solid eight-lane highway, one that can easily handle a large number of huge 18-wheel trucks transporting your strategy to its destination.

The nine most common Performance Management process problems

Over the years, .I've worked throughout the world with companies in different sectors on a variety of Strategy Execution topics. And while each company was unique, with their own cultures and products, the Strategy Execution process mistakes that they made were often identical.

Here's a list of the nine most common. You can make a quick self-assessment using the document provided on the website.

 Performance download 13. Score your Strategy Execution process – self-assessment.

Problem 1: Not easy. Most companies started off with a fairly straightforward, simple and pragmatic performance management process. But

they somehow succeeded in complicating it over time. But how?

Probably for one of the following reasons:

- A new manager arrived and implemented an approach that worked very well... in his/her former company.
- Corporate launched a new model and wanted everyone to follow it.
- Various consultants came (and went), each with their own tools and ideologies.
- Someone got a kick out of complex theoretical models.
- Someone wanted to create something completely new.
- Someone decided that everything needed to be integrated.
- ...And nobody eliminated outdated material.

Problem 2: Not understood by managers. You can have the best Strategy Execution process in the world, but if your managers don't get it, it's worthless.

Do you understand the Strategy Execution process in your organisation?

Problem 3: Not owned. Ownership of the Strategy Execution process is distributed among many different players.

Partial owners in large organisations often include the finance department, human resources, the strategy coordination team, internal consultants, several programme management offices (PMOs) and, last but not least, the managers themselves.

This fragmentation leads to lack of ownership for the global process. Most companies don't coordinate the activities spread across all these players. They all work in separate silos.

Problem 4: Not on the radar. Another disadvantage of the silo approach – apart from the lack of ownership – is the lack of visibility for the global process.

Separate, stand-alone, Strategy Execution topics such as budget discussions for new strategic initiatives, Key Performance Indicator (KPI) reviews or the selection of a new development programme, regularly make it to the boardroom table, but Strategy Execution as an activity doesn't. A missed opportunity.

Problem 5: Not to be changed. 'We have always done it this way' or 'This is what corporate wants' are phrases I have heard all too often – and probably you have too.

We all know that people don't like change. But for some reason (and I'm still trying to work out why – if you have the answer please let me know), this is especially true when it comes to managing performance. I've seen companies change their complete distribution model, but then panic at the mere thought of altering the timing of their budgeting cycle.

Problem 6: Not adapted to your needs. You don't need a cannon to kill a mosquito, but it might be useful to have a good tranquilizer gun if you want to transport a tiger.

Adapt your tools to your needs. All too often, companies forget this logic. A small business unit that is part of a big multinational does not always benefit from the fully-fledged corporate performance management process that works great for the other business units 10 times its size.

Harmonising doesn't mean copying without thinking.

Problem 7: Not measured (and therefore not known). Most companies today measure and monitor almost everything. Every part of the business has its own indicator.

But the Strategy Execution process itself remains a black box.

Crucial questions such as 'What percentage of our budget is allocated to strategic projects that have to secure our future?', 'What's the percentage of individual objectives linked to our strategy?' or 'What's the cost of our Strategy Execution process?' remain unanswered.

Problem 8: Not balanced. Most people prefer to spend their time on things they are already quite good at. You probably recognise this phenomenon.

Companies operate the same. I see organisations invest in those Strategy Execution process steps that are already quite developed, but then neglect the weaker ones – creating a vast difference between the different Strategy Execution building blocks.

Examples include a streamlined budgeting process but very poor strategy monitoring, solid objective setting but poor coaching skills, and interactive Balanced Scorecard discussions but poor initiative management.

And you know the saying: a chain is only as strong as its weakest link.

Problem 9: Not budget friendly. Performance management can be a very expensive process. Most companies forget to optimise the following three cost categories:

- *The managers' time investment.* Most managers lose time, and therefore money, by doing things that are not really needed (but asked anyway).
- *The activities of the process owners.* There are too many people keeping their jobs alive by continuing the complexity or adding even more. This also includes doing the same work in different department.
- *The impact of external consulting and training.* It's probably smart to get external advice and outsource performance management training activities.

  But watch out for the cost impact of these actions. The initial outlay might be very reasonable but the maintenance costs aren't. You could end up with a very cheap consultant but a massive total cost of ownership.

Twenty-seven guidelines to improve the Strategy Execution process in your organisation

Each company has its own unique strategy. And a unique strategy demands a unique Strategy Execution process. So, unfortunately, there is no magic recipe.

There are, however, proven ingredients you can include. And as head chef, it's your job to mix those ingredients into a unique recipe of success for your organisation.

Here is the cookbook with 27 proven ingredients. Some guidelines will be more difficult to implement then others, but all will contribute to the improvement of your Strategy Execution process.

You should regularly review these guidelines since new insights will emerge as new developments in your organisation take place. And these new insights will trigger fresh ideas to further improve the Strategy Execution process.

You can download a guideline overview to get you started. Use the list to evaluate the potential improvement impact of each guideline and define their importance for the next six months. You can repeat the exercise after four-to-six months in order to evaluate your progress and define new actions.

 Performance download 14. Boost your Strategy Execution process – guideline overview.

You can also turn the scoring exercise into an interesting workshop with your team.

 Performance download 15. Boost your Strategy Execution process – workshop format.

The first nine

Guideline 1: Know what your managers think about your Strategy Execution process

You probably knew, or know by now, that the manager plays a crucial role within the Strategy Execution process.

Make sure you know how s/he – that is, the average manager in your organisation – experiences your company's performance management process and evaluates their own Strategy Execution skills.

But don't assume you know the perception of all managers if you are one yourself. (That would be short-sighted, wouldn't it, as you are far better than the average manager).

Guideline 2: Integration should always be on your mind

It's difficult to design and implement a Balanced Scorecard approach, a new variable pay policy or a performance coaching training. But it's a real challenge to align all these elements into one coherent approach.

And yet the integration part is crucial.

So keep your current process in mind when you work on something new.

Be pro-active and try to predict possible conflicts that could arise between a new activity and the existing Strategy Execution process. The fit with the existing is as important as the new product itself.

Guideline 3: Select the right process owners

Here is a list of ideal character traits for process owners:
– A passion for performance.
– A high intrinsic motivation (read: 'self').
– The courage to challenge existing practices.
– The courage to admit a mistake and get on with it.
– The ability to take a manager's point of view.
– Client-orientation.
– Willingness to learn.
– Willingness to leave the comfort zone.

Guideline 4: Increase interaction between process owners

I highlighted the different Strategy Execution players in Chapter 2, of whom there are quite a few.

Sometimes, however, it seems as though they all come from a different planet – not ideal since everyone shares the same client – the manager.

But this does not necessarily mean that everyone needs to be involved in each activity. No, each player has, and maintains, his own particular role. But the different activities need to fit together like a jigsaw. And that will only happen if the interaction effort increases dramatically.

Guideline 5: Evaluate the process owners and their work

The performance management process owners are the guardians of a good performance management process. Their performance directly impacts the overall Strategy Execution performance, so make sure it is monitored and evaluated regularly.

Guideline 6: Define what's in and what's not

Strategy Execution will always be explained differently depending on who you talk to. As a company you want to avoid this – so you need to decide what's in and what's not. Have a clear vision on what is included in your Strategy Execution process and what isn't.

Topics that often create confusion include talent management, budgeting, project management, coaching and compensation.

Ultimately, you would like every manager in your organisation to be capable of defining your Strategy Execution process, at least on a conceptual level.

Guideline 7: Use a Strategy Execution framework

Once you have defined Strategy Execution within your organisation, it is useful to have an overall framework that captures your way of thinking.

Avoid the temptation to build a model that tries to fit all the strategy processes together. Stick to a flexible, easy to communicate, overall framework that allows for the integration of both existing and future models and activities for the different underlying building blocks.

And of course, I would suggest using the 8 as your framework. For more information, go to page chapter 1.

Guideline 8: Get the timing right

You can have all the right building blocks in place but this doesn't mean you're home free. Take a look at the order of the different activities. Are they set up logically?

Typical timing issues include support departments that have to deliver action plans before even having received input from the business departments, define annual individual objectives when the year is already well underway, and evaluate individuals before the year results are known.

These issues often occur when the two performance cycles are managed by different process owners (as is often the case), and tend to be worse in complex matrix structures.

So work on that timing. Your managers will be grateful.

Guideline 9: Have a clear vision on automation

It's a smart idea to automate the whole or part of your performance management process... but with care.

In many cases, the ambition to automate the process is the positive driver at the start of a Strategy Execution upgrade programme but the bottleneck the year after.

Let me give you an example.

Imagine that you want to automate part of the individual objective-setting process. You start by selecting a software package. You launch an expensive IT project to customise the solution. Nine months later, you receive many suggestions (and complaints) from managers regarding the user-friendliness of the software. After a closer look, you decide they are right and agree the underlying process needs to change. But that would demand, yet again, some quite extensive IT system changes. You find it inappropriate to launch a new IT project as the previous one was more expensive than anticipated. So you decide to wait.

I would suggest you either choose a standard software solution and change your process or postpone automation until you are 100 percent happy with the underlying process.

From 10-to-18

Guideline 10: Define your ambition for each building block

What do you expect from performance coaching? Where do you see initiative management three years from now?

You need to be able to answer these, and other questions.

A clear ambition for each Strategy Execution building block will help you define priorities and plan budgets. Make sure you:

    – Involve all stakeholders, make it a joint exercise.

- Create a global three-year vision.
- Build a detailed plan for the first year.
- Define how and when you will measure success.

Guideline 11: Define your guiding principles

Improving the Strategy Execution process isn't a precise science. You can't predict the outcome of your action plan. And you will need, more than once, to adjust your course to reach your desired maturity level.

It is smart to agree on some guiding principles, principles that will help you make those unexpected or unforeseen future decisions with clarity and consideration. They will help you and your team keep your vision and integrity on course.

Use them as a yardstick to measure your decisions, just as a company uses corporate values.

Guideline 12: Go slow but steady

The performance management process is at the core of an organisation. And even though it's not always that visible, the way strategy is executed is embedded in an organisation's culture. This means that changing the process demands changing people's behaviour, which takes enormous time and effort.

So don't try to change your Strategy Execution process in one go.

Be realistic, make smart choices, and with a few clever interventions, you will probably be able to significantly increase the maturity without overstretching the organisation.

Make it your challenge to identify these levers.

Guideline 13: Use a clever development approach

You will probably agree that most managers could benefit significantly from further Strategy Execution skills development. But there might be a problem. Research indicates that the majority believe they are better-than-average at defining and implementing strategy.

So, a subtle and clever development approach is needed. Don't push too much. Create plenty of 'voluntary' learning opportunities – for example, by offering non-mandatory, two-hour pick-and-choose sessions, combined with individual coaching, in place of compulsory two-day training.

Being clever about development doesn't mean that you accept poor performance. To illustrate that you are no soft touch, define and communicate the minimum skill requirements to all managers and then track them.

Guideline 14: Connect and learn
Look what others have done, or didn't do, and see if you can apply some of the learnings.

I started this chapter by indicating that each Strategy Execution process is unique. This is still valid. You can, however, save a substantial amount of time and money by learning from others. You still need to adapt what you learned to your specific situation, but it's much easier and smarter to adapt the tried and tested than to start from scratch.

From whom can you learn?

Make a list of people you know from both within and outside the organisation – and see how you can make the most of your network.

 Performance tip. Strategy Execution is a fast-developing knowledge field. New insights pop up every month. Take advantage of these new developments. Not all will be worthwhile or suit your needs but some will. Make it part of your routine to keep your Strategy Execution knowledge up-to-date.

Guideline 15: Review your meeting agenda
Most top teams spend less than an hour a month discussing strategy and its implementation. Management meetings – whether on a corporate, local or team level – are packed with short-term operational discussions. But an agenda full of urgent operational topics isn't an excuse to put aside the important strategic ones.

Want to do a little exercise?

Have a look at your management agenda from the last three-to-six months. Which elements of the 8 make it – or don't make it – onto the agenda? Evaluate the quality of the discussions and outcome. You can do the exercise for different hierarchical levels, compare results and use them as a great wake-up call for the others!

Guideline 16: Review the flight level of management discussions

Even if a topic makes it onto the management agenda, it can still be discussed in the wrong way. Why? Because the team gets caught up in the details.

Here's an example. Don't discuss project staffing in a management committee if it's the programme office's responsibility. Focus instead on the benefit tracking.

Changing flight levels proves to be initially very challenging as you will need substantially more time during the first few meetings to get through the agenda. So either book the extra time or delegate some operational topics to other committees.

After those first few meetings however, you will get into the routine and find yourself asking why you never did it before.

Guideline 17: Make a clean sweep

A large or medium-sized company often has lots of great methodologies, tools and systems that have been piling up over the years, or even decades, each (hopefully) having been useful at some point in time. Today, however, the Strategy Execution process looks like a house originally constructed as a simple two-bedroom building in the 1970s that has since seen the addition of 27 new rooms in 18 different styles.

Make an inventory of all existing material and sort them into three groups:

1. Essentials that you want to continue to use.
2. The non-essentials, but nice to haves.
3. And last, but not least... all the duplicates and outdated materials and methodologies.

After some thorough research in all departments, you could easily end up with three piles large enough to fill a boardroom table.

It also helps to get away from your desk and talk to managers in the field. They will give you valuable insights into the usability of the materials and methodologies – something you can't figure out just by looking at documents.

Guideline 18: Mind your language

Strategy Execution means too many things to different people.

Make a list of the keywords used within your organisation, agree on their definitions and stick to them. You can update them, but it's best done at the start of a new performance cycle.

The resulting lexicon should be widely available and used within the organisation. Integrate the definitions into your development programmes. Train your process owners. Make sure they understand the terminology and are able to explain keywords to others.

Don't worry if you can't agree on a definition immediately – being aware of the different perceptions is often already a huge step forwards.

One final comment: a lexicon becomes even more important in a multi-language environment.

From 19-to-27

Guideline 19: Build a great intranet site

More and more companies are increasingly using intranet sites as their primary, content rich, communication channel for a variety of topics. The intranet is also the perfect medium to promote Strategy Execution. Take a look at Chapter 3 for some tips and tricks on developing a best-in-class Strategy Execution intranet site.

Guideline 20: Create a best-in-class programme office

If you're serious about improving your Strategy Execution process, you will quickly end up with a long list of projects. Set up a professional PMO to manage them and let your programme management professionalism be an example to others.

Guideline 21: Always test first

Whether you introduce a new Strategy Execution methodology, tool or training session, make sure you test it thoroughly before implementation.

Run several pilots. Use waves of implementation. Here's why this is the best way forwards:

- *A small change can have a big effect.* You can't predict this at the beginning, even with the best preparation in the world. Therefore you should always do a dry run before implementation.
- *It takes time to make your initial idea simple.* Even if you get it right, there are always easier ways to do things. But you will only see this once you have started and actually tried to implement the idea.
- *It takes time for people to change their behaviour.*

 Performance tip: Be your own guinea pig. Before any launch, make sure you try everything yourself and are happy with the results.

Guideline 22: Lock the door

Once you find what works, make sure you freeze the chosen solution and make it the one and only. You don't want several different versions of the solution to start filtering their way into the organisation.

Guideline 23: Don't run before you can walk

Once you have what it takes, avoid adding new, unplanned additions along the way. Many companies that pass the first year successfully over-do it in the second year... and fail.

The risk also tends to be much higher when the initial team is changed mid-way.

Guideline 24: Watch the matrix (and I don't mean the movie!)

Matrix structures are common practice in many organisations, but do tend to have a very negative impact on the simplicity of processes... and that includes Strategy Execution. Most issues arise from mixed messages, timing mis-matches and power play between teams.

There's no need for you to start a crusade against matrix structures as they do have their advantages. But be aware of the various pitfalls.

To get a grip of the various matrix dimensions, you often need to focus first on the 'unwritten rules of the game'. You might find it helpful to put this topic on the agenda at the right level of your organisation as it can be a good starting point for defining and clarifying guidelines and managing interactions between divisions, departments, functional lines or teams.

Guideline 25: Measure success

Measuring and receiving feedback is one of the cornerstones of Strategy Execution. So, it's perfectly logical to apply these principles to the Strategy Execution process itself.

It's a good idea to build a simple dashboard. Start with just a few indicators. Define the improvement targets and measure progress on a regular basis. You might also want to consider a Strategy Execution benchmark which covers the key metrics. It will give your measurement approach a real boost.

 Performance tip: Don't stop at the template. Come up with best-practice examples. If you, the inventor, is unable to correctly use the newly designed document and come up with some great examples, what are the chances that others will be able to do it better?

Guideline 26: Build a Strategy Execution development platform

Strategy Execution is a relatively new, but rapidly growing, knowledge field. Today, most business schools include Strategy Execution in their curriculum, and some even make it a cornerstone of their teaching programme.

But this was not the case a few years ago, let alone a decade ago. Most managers over the age of 35 haven't had a formal education in Strategy Execution and therefore lack some of the basics. Some have caught up through reading, additional education or training courses, but most have not.

Don't leave your managers and process owners in the dark – provide them with the necessary development opportunities. Chapter 8 covers this extensively.

Guideline 27: Preach simplicity

I cannot emphasise enough the importance of keeping it simple – so I've added 'Preach simplicity' as the final guideline.

And now it's my turn to preach.

Make sure you always emphasise the importance of simplicity. Challenge Strategy Execution complexity at every opportunity. And use process simplicity as one of your Strategy Execution KPIs.

How to write a great performance story with the manager as the hero

A manager needs to collect, digest and integrate all available information, supporting material and documents and use the resulting bank of knowledge appropriately and effectively. Just like the production worker in a factory assembles all the individual components to produce a smooth-running machine.

So why not give your managers a helping hand?

Help them assemble the pieces by writing a 'performance story', a short guide that covers:

- The different steps of the Strategy Execution process.
- The manager's role in the process.
- The need and nice to haves.
- The available supporting material with best-in-class examples.
- The expected outcome.

Looks deceptively easy wouldn't you say? Well it does, but you might be in for a surprise. In my experience, 95 percent of individuals who did the exercise, including process owners, admitted afterwards to having found it very difficult. And most of them were also unhappy with the resulting quality.

The performance story forces you to be precise. You won't get away with saying '…and then you make your Balanced Scorecard' or 'In June you coach your people'. If you want a manager to use a Scorecard, you need to be very clear on the process to follow (or not to follow), the templates to use, the required level of detail, the quality evaluation criteria and so on. The same goes for the coaching example: you need to be direct and state clearly if people should use a model or not, or the type of training to follow, the coaching tips available and if there is the possibility of using an external coach or not.

And while you might be able to answer all these questions, it can be a real challenge to reach that all-important single vision. Different points of view will become very apparent and need to be discussed as you can have only one storyline.

Remember: writing a performance story is one of the best ways to harmonise your Strategy Execution process. You can download an example from the website.

 Performance download 16. Write a great performance story – an example.

It's great to transform the exercise into a group workout. That way, everyone jointly experiences the complexity of the process. It's a great eye-opener seeing the differences between participants. You can download a workshop format to get you started.

 Performance download 17. Write a great performance story – workshop format.

Here are six proven tips to write a great performance story:
1. *Use instructional language.* You want individuals to take a specific action – so use a clear instructional style:
   – Refer directly to the reader.
   – Use clear language.
   – Keep it short and to the point.
   – Use short phrases.
   – Include a call for action.

2. *Use a sales pitch.* You want to convince people to do something, to take ownership. So there also needs to be something in it for them. Highlight the benefits. Tackle the 'What's in it for me?' question head-on.

3. *Make a clear distinction between nice to have and need to have.* Even after you have thrown away all the outdated and useless stuff, you will still have lots of material left. Make sure you separate the crucial bits from the nice to haves.

4. *Explain to your managers how to use the story.* Don't just hand it over. Explain why you developed it and how it will serve their purpose. Do this before you start any other actions such as training.

5. *Indicate a change if there is one.* When your Strategy Execution process changes, make sure you align all related material including intranet sites, templates and training courses. And don't forget to update the story. Indicate the change clearly and organise a separate communication.

6. *Show best-practices instead of empty templates.* All too often, managers receive empty templates with a request to start using them. But where is the value? If you want managers to work with a template, provide at least one, or preferably several, high-quality examples. Remember: one good example works better than 10 empty templates. And if you can't produce a good example, you probably aren't ready to launch.

Four frequently asked questions about performance stories

Question 1: Can my company have more than one performance story? Yes. If the process is different for different groups, there can be another story. However, the number of stories is a good indication of the complexity of your Strategy Execution process. And as said before, the more complex it is, the more chance it has of failure.

Question 2: Can I change a story? Yes. Over time, you or your colleagues construct better ways of doing things and the story needs to be adapted. So it is not a question of 'can' but a question of 'must'.

When you change things, it is also important to explain why and how you made the changes, as well as what this means for the manager. *Question 3: Do I need to write a story for the whole cycle?* No. Focus on the areas that need the most attention. The rest can always be added later.

Question 4: Do I need to be the process owner to write it? No. Every manager can benefit from writing the story. It is often a good basis to have an open discussion with the process owner to create a platform for change. In the end, your organisation should consolidate the stories, but as a starting point it's not necessary.

A view on Strategy Execution by Alan Maxwell, Vice President Human Resources, Lockheed Martin

What do you consider to be the most important Strategy Execution challenge for an executive team?

I believe that the biggest challenge is to bring the strategy to life in the hearts and minds of all employees – the ones who will need to take action to get things done. In order to tackle this challenge, the executive team needs a solid strategy communication approach. Getting the strategy communication right is a challenge in itself. A million things can go wrong. Luckily, there are quite a few best practices available.

Here's my list of communication pointers:

1. A strategy story needs a compelling business case that creates enthusiasm and inspires people.
2. A strategy story needs to be simple and with a high repeatability factor. Employees need to be able to pick it up easily and be able to repeat the story vividly at the kitchen table to their families.
3. People need to be able to relate to a strategy story. Great strategy stories make it easy for employees to fit in.
4. Keep your strategy story consistent. Stick to your message and make sure other do too. By the time you have possibly got bored of telling the same story over and over again, you will have probably reached

only 10 percent of your target population. So keep repeating the same message.

5. Make your financial drivers and levers transparent.
6. Invest heavily in awareness creation. And by this, I am not so much talking about money, but about time investment from senior management. A mere fly-by – where the executive just shows up and leaves after five minutes – won't do the trick. S/he needs to land and actually get out of the plane.
7. The top executives should be the communication role models. They have to set the example.
8. An organisation should constantly invest in building great communication skills. This includes looking for best practices inside and outside of the organisation, providing the right training and putting tools in place.
9. Never forget: communication involves two sides. On one side, there's the person who throws the ball, while, on the other side, there is the one who needs to catch it. All too often, the first player is ready to throw the second ball without first knowing if the receiver has caught the first one. A great communicator doesn't limit her/himself to great throwing alone. S/he makes sure that the first ball has been caught and follows through to see what the next step should be. Don't base your communication rhythm on your own understanding but on that of your audience.

What Strategy Execution advice would you give to an ambitious manager?

Young managers with the ambition to excel at Strategy Execution have quite a few interesting development challenges in front of them. However, ideally, they should not embark on the learning journey by themselves. Any organisation that is convinced of the importance of Strategy Execution should support their key talents by offering plenty of development opportunities including coaching, job rotation, formal and on-the-job training.

Here are the Strategy Execution development areas that I believe a performance-driven young manager should focus on:

1. ***Shift from expert to influencer.*** Be aware that your agenda will look quite different at a senior level. Your focus will shift from 'doing the work and being recognised as the expert' to coaching others getting things done in the best possible way. This not only demands a new skill set that includes coaching and teaching, but also a mind shift. And the latter can be more difficult to achieve than one might think as most people like their expert recognition and find it difficult to give up.

2. ***Surround yourself with the best.*** As your role shifts from 'expert/doer' to 'influencer/coach/teacher', you will need to surround yourself with the right people. Learn to recognise talent and practise putting those people in the limelight. Remember: you will be successful when they are successful.

3. ***Build active listening skills.*** It's not what you say that is the most important, but what you hear. But it seems that quite a few young managers forget this crucial management rule and spend most of their time talking and ignoring the listening part. By acting this way, they lose out on two crucial Strategy Execution success factors: collecting valuable feedback and increasing buy-in. So make sure you build your active listening skills as a key strength and be sure to apply them all the time.

4. ***Align what you say with what you do.*** Each individual has a unique personality and set of competencies. Make sure you know what your gifts are and use them to build your career. Focus on your strengths and build from there. Don't try to be someone that you are not. Be sincere. When people see that you are comfortable and happy with what you do, you will be much more successful.

5. ***Stay hungry.*** Have a mindset that is always tuned to continuous improvement. My coach once told me: *"If your feet are not moving, you will get knocked over"*. Make sure you keep moving forwards, even if the steps are very small. This doesn't mean you shouldn't

aim for the big, long-term goals any more. They remain important as well. But you do want to keep a 'doing' attitude and an improvement orientation in the short-term matters as well. Set yourself daily, weekly and monthly goals and evaluate honestly how well you did. It will keep your feet moving and get you into the habit of getting things done.

6. *Always look for feedback.* It's one of the best ways to boost your learning curve. If people don't offer their feedback, make sure you ask for it.

7. *Understand and build employee engagement.* The emotional component is a crucial performance driver. People who are emotionally connected will take the extra step not because they have to, but because they want to. But the emotional connection is often overlooked when looking for ways to improve performance. And that's a shame. Imagine what you could achieve with your team if everyone is engaged and ready to go all the way to get the strategy executed.

8. *Learn to influence without the hierarchical advantage.* Organisational structures are much less hierarchical than they used to be. And as executing strategy doesn't stop at the border of a department or division, getting things done without the leverage of being the boss becomes more difficult. The fear factor – seen in someone who will do something because they fear their job or bonus – disappears. Therefore, it is important that a leader possesses strong soft skills and is able to get people onboard without needing to use a whip. So a young manager needs to learn how to get things done from people that don't report to them. And this demands a much more sophisticated set of soft skills. Start building them today.

Based on your experience, what's a classic Strategy Execution mistake?
The first one that pops into my mind is 'not listening to the individuals

who are actually doing the work'. They are the ones who will always be able to provide the best available Strategy Execution feedback.

The second one is what I call 'island behaviour'. And the result of this island behaviour is that organisations stop doing the things they shouldn't stop doing. They:

- Stop learning from others. In other words, they stop looking beyond the company walls and focus solely on their own organisation.
- Stop challenging what you are doing believing that you will reach the finish line.

Looking at Strategy Execution from a 'human resources department' point of view, what is the most important topic for you?

Strategy Execution is the key to almost everything in an organisation. It should therefore get all the attention it deserves. I often simplify the execution challenge as the balance between 'the big dream' on the one hand and the 'tenacity to get it executed' on the other hand. Execution is nothing more than the long march towards the big dream. And the crucial role for the leaders in the organisations is to:

- Motivate everyone to keep going.
- Align everyone to walk at the same pace so that no one is left behind or is too much in front.
- Walk closely together and create interaction.
- Don't lose things on the way.
- And last, but not least, to have the strength to relentlessly say no when arriving at a promising looking side road.

PERFORMANCE TAKEAWAYS

- The Strategy Execution process is the Strategy Execution backbone.
- Improving your Strategy Execution process demands courage and persistence.
- Use the guidelines provided to evaluate and improve the quality of your Strategy Execution process.
- Write a great performance story that is compelling and clear-cut. And bring all performance management process information together on one page. It's one of the best ways to harmonise your Strategy Execution process.
- And if you need to remember just one thing from this chapter... it's *keep it simple!*

And the answer is? 'Simplify: From 100-to-1 in less than 3 years'.
By now you will probably have figured out the title. It takes time to simplify things and you should not rush into it. The execution process is at the heart of an organisation and closely connected to a company's culture.

A three-year time frame is a good outlook for a large or medium-sized company. It takes smaller companies less time.

Furthermore, 100 does not mean the same for every company. Each company has a different starting point, some being more mature than others.

Why not start with a Strategy Execution benchmark to see how your implementation capability compares to your closest competitors?

CHAPTER VII

Challenge 5: Initiate: How to eat an elephant with 5 people

"You can have anything you want –
you just can't have everything you want"
– Anonymous

"Plans are only good intentions unless they immediately
degenerate into hard work"
– Peter Drucker

"Initiative prioritisation doesn't mean distributing all
available resources to all known projects"
– Volker Voigt

Initiative management is probably my favourite part of the 8. It's the point where resources are added to the magic strategy formula, where organisational performance meets individual performance and where strategy translates into practice or remains on paper forever.

Initiative management challenges you to combine strategic and operational skills, to balance the short- and long-term. To summarise, initiative management separates the strategy tourists from the performance heroes.

In the previous chapter, I compared your Strategy Execution process with a highway. Continuing with this metaphor, initiative management is the fleet of trucks that you use to deliver your strategy to its final destination. They are your main strategy transporters.

This chapter will help you to assess the current initiative management quality and provide you with 32 tips to make improvements.

Some facts and figures about projects and programmes

- Research from Palladium, McKinsey and *the performance factory* shows that:
  - Companies spend billions every year on the 'wrong' projects.
  - Less than 50 percent of all projects are truly aligned to a company's strategy.
  - Only one in seven projects add value beyond 'staying even', in that they strengthen the company's competitive position, differentiate the product offer or create unique capabilities.
  - Companies that align initiatives to strategic objectives can achieve up to 20 percent savings.
  - Companies that actively manage their initiative portfolio can add up to 30 percent more value.
  - Almost 40 percent of all managers believe that the strategic initiatives in their company are staffed with the wrong people.
- Strategic themes, objectives, measures and targets represent *what* your organisation wants to accomplish, whereas strategic initiatives represent *how*. Initiatives push an organisation into motion – away from the current state and towards an ambition. Initiatives ignite action and aim to close the current performance gaps. They are a collection of carefully selected programmes and projects, operating outside of the day-to-day business, and reinforcing each

other to help the organisation reach its targeted performance.

- Project, programme and portfolio management. What's the difference? Nobody likes boring definitions and I'm sure you don't either. But the distinctions are important. All three have a definitive role to play within the initiative management process. And therefore you don't want to mix them up. So here are two easy-to-remember definitions to keep them apart:
  - Think of projects as the atoms of Strategy Execution – the low-level, well-defined packages of work that enable it to function. Think of programmes as the molecules of strategic intent, in which specific clusters of project atoms are tightly bound to one another by technical and organisational bonds to yield higher-level strategic deliverables. The planned portfolio is simply the complete set of projects and programmes that have been selected to execute an organisation's strategic intent. (Adapted from Morgan, Leveitt and Malek).
  - Project management is like juggling with three balls of time, cost and quality. Programme management is like a troupe of circus performers standing in a circle, each juggling three balls, occasionally swapping them around. Initiative management puts all your circus acts together, carefully organised to maximise the number of visitors. (Adapted from G. Reiss).
- When you do your resource planning, think about the IBM study that revealed that people working on one project only reach around 60 percent of their maximum productivity. With two projects underway, their productivity increases to around 70 percent (with some efficiency loss during the switching). And when the project count increases to three, productivity drops to under 50 percent, and with more than four projects, to less than 30 percent.

Why do most managers struggle with initiative management?

Research from *the performance factory* reveals not only that initiative management is the weak spot in the Strategy Execution chain; it also shows us that most managers find this execution activity to be the most challenging.

They do so for a number of reasons, such as:

- Initiative management builds on the results of something else. When the previous step delivers poor quality, it's very difficult to get it back on track.
- It crosses the traditional silos so the ownership is often blurred.
- It requires sound decision-making – decisions which are not always yours to take.
- It's often in addition to the daily work.

Thirty-two tips organised according to five initiative management fundamentals

Let's get started right away. Here's a list of 32 proven tips, organised around five initiative fundamentals, that will help you master initiative management in your organisation. The five clusters are:

1. Collect, select and prioritise the right initiatives.
2. Optimise your resource allocation and planning.
3. Develop your project managers.
4. World-class project and programme management.
5. Manage your strategic initiative portfolio.

You might want to start with the checklist available for download from the website. You could also turn the scoring exercise into an interesting workshop with your team. There are also some guidelines or you can go straight to reading the tips.

 Performance download 18. Best-in-class initiative management – a checklist.

 Performance download 19. Best-in-class initiative management – workshop format.

Fundamental 1: Collect, select and prioritise the right initiatives

The first thing to do is to gather all the possible initiative ideas. Most of the time, there will be no shortage of ideas from your creative sources, your team or organisation, so spend the time tapping into them.

Once you've gathered all possible initiatives to support your strategy, it's time to make tough choices. Limited resources will force you to weed through all the initiatives, prioritise them and pick those that best fit your strategy *and* budget.

Here are some tips to help you with this process:

Tip 1: Aim for 100 percent connection. It's crucial to link your initiatives to your strategy. If the cascade exercise has been done properly, you should have identified a list of initiatives and considered their contribution to your strategy at length. You should also feel satisfied that the list is correct and that there has been a solid ideation to be as creative as possible.

But what if you're not sure?

Draw a simple matrix. Put your strategy themes on one axis and your initiatives on the other. Look out for 'blanc' spots. Don't be satisfied with putting just X's. Debate assumptions with your team and don't stop until you all feel that there's a 100 percent fit.

Be aware: you can tie almost every project to every initiative if you have enough imagination. But that's not the objective here, is it? Don't be satisfied until you have challenged and debated all assumptions.

The matrix offers an extra value: it not only helps you to find the white spots or stimulate discussions, but it will also prove to be a great communication tool at a later stage.

Tip 2: Do more than just mandatory projects. You've carefully selected a portfolio of project ideas which support your strategy, but a tremendous backlog of so-called mandatory projects made it on the list as well.

You know the ones – projects which relate to regulations, tax changes or compliance. And they all seem to have top priority. And you know from experience that there are always new mandatory projects waiting in the wings to get on the priority list as well.

So what about your strategic project?

While most of the topics from the so-called 'mandatory' project are in fact mandatory, there's almost always room for interpretation on how they need to be implemented. All too often, managers use the mandatory elements to push the project higher up the project list and inflate the project budget.

So make sure you challenge them and don't let mandatory projects block your Strategy Execution.

Tip 3: Perform initial project management tasks first. Clarify the scope, fix deadlines and understand drivers before you set initiative priorities. Make sure you have a process in place involving experienced project managers who can deliver high-level resource estimates in a short time frame. These carefully considered estimates are essential to selecting the right initiatives.

Tip 4: Watch out for pet projects. Everyone has their favourite projects. I'm sure you do too. And it shouldn't be a problem. Unless, of course, it clouds the judgement and the selection process ceases to be objective.

Tip 5: Don't try to do everything and end up doing nothing. Be selective. Reality shows that an organisation can absorb fewer projects than most executives think. Better to hold off until some projects reach the next phase.

Prioritisation doesn't mean distributing all available resources to all known projects.

Rank your initiatives and pick the top 30 percent for immediate launch. Put the rest on hold. Repeat the exercise after three-to-six months. The picture will look different as new initiatives arise and projects in process have advanced to different stages.

Tip 6: Costs = 80, benefits = 0. When you prioritise new and existing projects, consider only the remaining costs and benefits. Projects which are 80 percent completed have 80 percent sunk costs. But usually all the benefits are yet to come. Focus on these projects that are 80 percent of the way there. Finish them and enjoy the benefits.

Fundamental 2: Optimise your resource allocation and planning

Once you are confident that you have selected the strategic initiatives to propel your strategy to performance, it's time to allocate the human and financial resources. Here are some tips to help achieve this:

Tip 7: Align initiatives and budget. The initiative management and budget processes run separately in most companies. Make sure the financials are the same at both ends. Here are three points to watch out for:

- *Make sure your initiatives are included in the budget.* At their outset, most initiatives are nothing more than a few lines in a PowerPoint presentation. At best, they have a rough plan and a high-level budget estimate. Avoid surprises and include them all in your budget.
- *Make sure your initiatives do not remain budget bubbles.* Initiatives shouldn't remain inactive solely as reserves of money to fund managers' pet projects. Either detail them or cut them and make it a team decision to reallocate money where it fits best.
- *Make sure your initiatives remain within the budget.* When the going gets tough, management can be tempted to move in for the easy kill and reduce, reallocate or cut the budget of one or more strategic initiatives. And while this might solve a short-term burning issue, it undermines the future of the company. Kaplan and Norton, the founding fathers of Strategy Execution, promote the use of a separate expenditure category to fund all strategic projects and by doing so avoiding the issue.

Tip 8: Reward the long-term. Let me be clear. Short-term focus is important. It can even be your only focus when the going gets tough.

But that's not the point I want to make. Problems arise when managers constantly favour the short-term, no matter what the economic situation. These problems are often induced or reinforced by a reward system.

When this happens, the strategy exercise becomes a budget (read 'bonus') negotiation. And managers search to remove the risk in order to earn their next bonus. This often means that they neglect great initiatives and/or opportunities considering them too high risk, not for the company but for the achievement of their annual bonus.

Tip 9: Apply the '95 percent rule'. Depending on who you ask, a project budget, a timeline or a degree of difficulty, might be viewed quite differently. It's a question of risk-awareness by the estimator.

Ask your estimator the following question: 'What would it cost in terms of budget and schedule to have a 95 percent chance to realise the benefits within the planned budget and schedule?'.

Most people will, depending on their risk-awareness profile, review their plan (sometimes drastically) and provide you with a more realistic estimate. If all projects are estimated using the 95 percent rule, the risk is taken into account.

Tip 10: Make your capacity plan early. The successful realisation of an initiative is closely related to the quality of the staffing. Knowing this, ensure that your capacity plan is made early in the game. And be realistic. You are sure to find resource bottlenecks, but as you started early, you will still have time to find countermeasures.

> *"I have never seen a successful project run by a bad project manager"*

Tip 11: Appoint an architect to monitor the implementation. Imagine you are building a house. You have all the blueprints, made a great plan and all the contractors are ready to start. And then you go on holiday, right?

What's the chance that things will get done without a substitute to oversee the project?

Make sure you have a caretaker!

Tip 12: Ensure resources are, and stay, committed. Not every project has the same priority in each department. A project that's on the 'A list' in sales could well be insignificant to the marketing department. But without the marketing intervention, the sales team won't be able to pull it off. And a well-intentioned commitment – a 'yes' – at the beginning of a project could easily turn into a 'no' as other projects become higher priority. So when the marketing input is needed on the sales project, there are no resources available.

Make sure that doesn't happen to your project. Small actions can help keep everyone committed to your project and make all the difference between success and failure.

Keep all parties involved from the beginning and throughout the project, even if their intervention is minimal and planned for the final stages.

Tell them regularly about the importance of their interventions.

Build in a financial lever. Add an individual performance objective.

Tip 13: Assign your best project managers to your strategic projects. Don't use project size as the only element for planning staff resources. I'm always surprised when I see great project managers working on very large, but relatively risk-free, three-year 'maintenance' projects, while strategic projects are assigned to mediocre staff or outside consultants.

Put your money where your mouth is. Commit your best resources to the projects that deliver your company's future performance. Afraid to move staff between projects? Read the next tip.

Tip 14: Don't be afraid to reassign a project manager. 'He cannot be moved', 'She's worked for three years on that project. Reassigning her would be a disaster', 'But he wants to continue'.

Ever heard these arguments before?

Probably. And yes, you will lose some vital knowledge, and yes, it will take some time for a new project manager to get up to speed. But that's the micro view. As an organisation, you want the macro view. And with that helicopter view, you might be far better off reassigning.

There are no excuses to keep your best project managers blocked on those large, steady projects. Take a look at any consulting organisation: they are able to change project managers in a matter of weeks when clients demand it.

And for the record: good project managers love the rotation. It boosts their learning curve. Yet another benefit.

Performance exercise. The right project manager on the right project.

Make two lists. The first one ranks your projects. You can choose your own ranking criteria but avoiding using only the size of a project as the gauge. Also include, for example, strategic importance and complexity.

The second list ranks your project managers with the best on top. Is there a match between the two lists? Did you staff your best project managers on your most important projects? If not, take action.

You want to perform this exercise on a regular, even quarterly, basis. You will see that while the strategic importance of a project stays the same (unless you revise your portfolio), the project complexity indicator, for example, will shift as a project enters or leaves a certain maturity phase. Over time, your project managers ranking will change as well.

Tip 15: 'IT' is always late. And IT is often not to blame. But regardless as to whether the delay is caused by incomplete specification, changed business needs, underestimation of complexity, technical challenges, interfaces to other systems, lack of resources or problems with the out-sourcer, it nevertheless remains a delay.

So get over the good guy/bad guy discussions with IT and tighten that relationship. Set up a professional, high-quality, business-IT partnership and tackle one of the main reasons why projects are delayed head-on.

Fundamental 3: Develop your project managers

I don't need to tell you that a project manager can make or break a successful project. In fact, I've never seen a successful project run by a bad project manager. Project managers are key to project success.

So make sure you give your project managers – and their skills development – the attention they deserve as they are both key to your initiative management success.

Tip 16: *Project managers need hard AND soft skills*. A project manager isn't a one-trick pony. A project manager needs to master a variety of skills, not all of which are related to technical project management activities such as planning, risk management, reporting or financial control. They also include soft skills, which for some projects are actually more valuable than hard skills.

So make sure you put soft skills such as communication, negotiating and coaching on your project managers' development agenda.

Tip 17: *A PMI certification doesn't do the trick*. All too often, project managers' skills development is reduced to 'get your PMI certification'.

And while having PMI (Project Management Institute) credentials, a PRINCE2 (Projects IN Controlled Environments) accreditation or a IPMA (International Project Management Association) certification, is undeniably useful, it should not be the development cornerstone.

Tip 18: *Offer your project managers an interesting career path.*
If you are serious about project management, make sure you can offer project managers a great future within your organisation. A professional career path is a fantastic lever to help you hire, motivate, advance and reward your project managers.

Tip 19: *Projects: a great opportunity to develop future leaders.*
Appoint high potential staff to your strategic projects. It will give them valuable exposure to a new environment, offer them an interesting challenge and provide a fast-track learning experience.

And although most high potentials will more than have the ability to manage a crucial project, do make sure they have the right (read 'soft *and* hard') project management skills. You don't want to ignore Tip 16. If they do have the right skills, a project assignment is a win-win situation.

Tip 20: Evaluate your project managers regularly. Each project has its own dynamics outside of the operational cycle that drives day-to-day business.

Make sure you follow the logic of the project when it comes to evaluating performance.

Don't wait until the end-of-year formal evaluation. Evaluate project managers at the end of each important phase. If you wait too long, you will have to chase project members who have long moved on to other assignments and clients who have forgotten all about the details.

This doesn't mean, however, that you have to cancel the end-of-year performance review. On the contrary. But regular reviews will provide you with the high-quality feedback you need for a proper evaluation at the year-end.

Tip 21: Build a community. You can find project managers spread throughout the organisation. I call them 'organisational nomads'. They travel from project-to-project, they don't belong to a certain silo and don't report to the same boss. But they do all practise the same job, face similar challenges and generally have the same career concerns.

Why not bring them altogether on a regular basis?

Give them the opportunity to create a sense of belonging that extends beyond their current project and let them share ideas with like-minded individuals. Not every week however, since your nomads need their freedom. But organising a lunch or an activity on a bi/monthly basis is a smart thing to do.

Tip 22: Make sure you have the right HR expertise on board. A professional, structured development approach for your initiative management demands specific skills and knowledge. Make sure you have – or get – that specific expertise onboard. It will save you time and money.

Fundamental 4: World-class project and programme management

There is so much to say on the topic. There has been much already said on the topic. Project and programme management are mature business activities that have been around for quite some time now.

With the help of Volker Voigt, initiative management specialist, I've selected seven tips that will help you overcome some of the more persistent project and programme management problems. There are also more project management resources available for download.

 Performance download 20. Interesting project management resources.

Tip 23: Adopt a project standard. Research shows a high positive correlation between the use of a standardised project management methodology and project success.

Be careful, however. 'Standardised' does not mean 'standard'. Make sure you adapt terminology, project life and tools to your needs and project culture. If not, it can do more harm than good.

Tip 24: Provide a project starter kit. Each project needs to actually start. And it will go through the same activities and possibly the same launch mistakes as all the others.

Give your project managers and members a kick-start with a starter kit: a collection of steps, a to-do list, tips and examples that will help them succeed with that crucial first step in the project life cycle. Make sure the kit isn't overly technical and do include some tips on the unwritten project management rules of your organisation. And remember: the more project launches you do, the more you learn and the better your starter kit becomes.

I would suggest you organise a launch meeting to run through the starter kit whenever a larger programme starts or several projects are due to start within the same time frame (a few weeks).

Tip 25: Use collaboration and information management tools wisely. Maybe you know the expression 'a fool with a tool is still a fool'. Well, it's also a valid one in the project and programme management environment.

Don't think that tools will solve all your problems. Be careful that your tool isn't a gadget, creating pleasure for the happy few who selected it but a pain for the others who have to work with it.

Tools can boost productivity, but need to be treated with care. Take an informed, rational decision.

Tip 26: Avoid immortal projects. This is a tip about project closure as many projects make a bid for eternal life.

Mysteriously, projects – temporary activities with *ad hoc* staffing – transform themselves gradually into jobs – structured activities with fixed staff. And as a result they keep going and going. (I'm tempted to add another 'and going' but I'm sure you got my point). And before you know it, the whole organisation is overwhelmed with a host of never-ending corporate initiatives.

Plan your exit strategy. Define upfront when and how the mission will end and capture the benefits in the day-to-day business operations.

Remember: it's easier to close projects when the organisation has a clear career path for project managers and can offer other challenging assignments.

Tip 27: Establish rituals. Human beings like habits. They provide structure and comfort. Use this knowledge to your advantage. Develop your own project and programme rituals. Keep this in mind when you are deciding on reporting structures, formats and steering committees. Anything that is repetitive helps ritual building.

Tip 28: Achieve results, not phases. Have you ever seen those impressive wallpaper-sized project plans decorating the director's office, boasting how well the project is under control? I guess so. And when you looked closely, you saw the project plan covered hundreds of activities neatly structured into phases such as 'the preparation phase', 'the implementation phase' and 'the testing phase'. And you probably asked yourself: 'But where are the benefits?'.

Most project plans are task-oriented when they should actually be results-driven. The difference always shows in the project plan. Make sure that all activities in your project plan show a clear link with your deliverables. And use the progress towards these deliverables, not the action steps, as your real progress indicator.

Fundamental 5: Manage your strategic initiative portfolio

Project and programme management are temporary activities put in place to close a specific performance gap. But once that gap is (hopefully) closed, you will start closing another one, as the competitive battlefield is constantly in motion. So no matter what, there will always be the need to perform the various initiative management activities. Here are some tips to build permanent capability.

Tip 29: Create a permanent strategy office. And let the office take primary responsibility to manage your initiative portfolio. It's something more and more companies do. Download some extra tips to set up your own.

 Performance download 21. How to set up a strategy office – tips.

Tip 30: Build the right culture. You probably know project traffic lights – those three-colour caution signals often used in project status reporting. Well, it's your company culture that defines how a red traffic light should be read. It varies from 'I need help from the steering committee to solve project problems' to 'I'm so sorry. I tried to hide the problem for as long as possible but now everything is in a total mess!'.

As long as you encourage project managers to address risks before they become issues, you still have a chance of manoeuvring the project out of the danger zone. However, project managers, operating in a culture that accuses and prosecutes problem identifiers, will conceal risks. So your company culture has quite an impact on your project risk management.

Tip 31: Develop your decision-taking capability. Initiative management demands solid decision-taking skills at all levels. From selecting the right initiative to allocating resources, it all comes down to taking decisions. You need to be good at it. Here are some simple tricks I often use:

- *Provide options.* Useful when a group needs to consider a decision. Make sure you do your homework and detail each option.
- *Make a yes/no list.* Useful when you need to force a decision. Use it at the end of a steering committee, capture the outcome and communicate the decisions.
- *Use a sounding board to prepare a decision.* Useful when you have limited time with the final decision-makers. Select the right players, those who are trusted advisers of the final decision-makers.

 Performance tip. Remember this one next time you take a decision. Best-selling author Paul C. Nutt did extensive research on decision making for his book *Why Decisions Fail.* He found that more than 50 percent of all decisions fail. They are either quickly abandoned, partially implemented or never adopted at all. Eighty-one percent of all managers pushed their decisions through persuasion and edict. And only seven percent were based on long-term priorities. Despite these shocking figures, 91 percent of the managers in Nutt's study rated themselves as exceptional decision-makers.

Tip 32: Initiative management as a strategic project. Are you serious about developing initiative management as a core competence? If the answer is yes, set up a new initiative called 'Initiative management as a core competence in our organisation'.

A crucial next step, but almost always forgotten

You defined a great strategy. You cascaded your company strategy into objectives for the different organisational units, and you selected, prioritised and staffed all your strategic initiatives. So that's it, right?

All too often, unfortunately, that's where the cascade stops and the 8 breaks down.

But what's missing?

There is no link between the project/programme deliverables and the benefits with the individual objectives. Let's be clear. This doesn't mean that the individuals involved don't have individual objectives – as in most cases they do. But in most cases they only cover the day-to-day activities or at best say something like 'Work on project X'.

Don't make that mistake. You've come this far. Integrate those project milestones, deliverables and benefits (!) into the objectives of the individuals involved.

How?

Make a list of all the deliverables. Assign one owner per deliverable (not two or three) and add the realisation of this benefit to the list of individual objectives of that individual. Always aim for the best possible connection between individual and organisational performance.

In case I haven't yet convinced you, here are three benefits of linking your strategic initiatives with individual objectives:

1. *A great way to check the realism of your projects.* A performance-driven individual will not accept objectives that don't seem attainable.

2. *Increase the performance of individuals working on your project.* If you have already read Chapter 3, you will know that individual goals, when accepted, increase performance.

3. *A great way to secure project resources from other departments.* There's a world of difference between 'Yes, okay, our department will do it' and 'Yes, Mike and Angela will work on that project as we have agreed and I have translated your project objectives into their individual objectives and got their commitment'. Making the

link with individual performance helps secure commitment. The more your project depends on resources out of your direct control, the more benefits you will reap.

A view on Strategy Execution by Jean-Francois Van Kerckhove, Vice President Corporate Strategy, eBay

What do you consider to be the most important Strategy Execution challenge for an executive team?

I believe that there are three core prerequisites for successful Strategy Execution. Without these requirements in place, execution is compromised from the start. Unfortunately, they are often taken for granted when they shouldn't be. The three prerequisites are:

1. Have a clear strategy.
2. Empower teams to successfully execute on the strategy.
3. Foster a culture and systems that root out status quo or non-execution.

Let's look at them in more detail:

1. **Have a clear strategy**. It is critical to have executive alignment concerning the strategic imperatives – the execution North Star. But it is also critical to have alignment and shared awareness about the main foundations of the strategy. Key questions to ask at the executive level are:
   - Do we share aspirations and explicit goals?
   - Is our strategy based on explicit and shared awareness of our beliefs regarding the external environment and our internal capabilities?
   - Do we agree on the company values?
   - What is the best management philosophy to run the business?
   - Without clear alignment on these crucial elements, a company may exhibit schizophrenic behaviours when it comes to executing strategy.

2. **Empower teams to successfully execute on the strategy.** To set up an organisation and its employees for success, it is important for

employees to understand, and as much as possible, shape the 'what' of the strategy, to understand the 'why' behind the strategy, and be given the power and freedom to decide on and successfully execute on the 'how' of the Strategy Execution. Communication, involvement and empowerment are critical and can't be underestimated. These are critical building blocks to enable the unlocking of passion and higher performance. At the same time, empowerment only goes so far in the absence of the necessary talent. Maintaining an objective perspective on talent needs and ensuring that the right talent is deployed is a condition *sine qua non*.

3. **Foster a culture and systems that root out status quo or non-execution.** The flip side of effective Strategic Execution is non-execution or irrelevant execution. Some specific actions can be taken to mitigate the risk of non-execution by removing or preventing systems and cultural barriers.

   From *a systems point of view*, it's important to prevent dilution of effort, remove organisational frictions and have warning systems in place to act rapidly in case of poor or non-performance. Specific solutions could include:
   - Focus on specific, measurable priorities with a tie back to corporate level objectives.
   - Set up clear responsibility lines.
   - Organise as much as possible around small, agile, accountable and empowered teams while minimising dependencies.
   - Establish clear monitoring processes to maintain accountability and visibility.
   - Enable fluid allocation of resources.

   From *a cultural point of view*, it is important to encourage team empowerment and accountability in a context of collaboration and openness. This should be reflected in the corporate values, role modelled top down and reinforced through compensation and performance evaluation systems.

What Strategy Execution advice would you give to an ambitious manager?

– Provide clear direction and objectives to your team in light of the strategic priorities of the business.

– Empower/challenge your team to shape and own the 'how'.

– Make sure your team has all the tools, skills and resources to succeed.

– Shield your team from distractions and from becoming too reactive to outside interferences.

– Don't forget that it is a multi-step 'game' – treat your team well, help them grow, and figure out if you are running a sprint or a marathon.

Based on your experience, what's a classic Strategy Execution mistake?

I'm not sure that there is one classic 'mistake'. I would consider 'mistakes' as the flip side of my recommendations above.

One belief that I would like to call out, is that the nature of the execution of a strategic priority should not come at the expense of the values of an organisation, but should be reinforcing the values. Tolerating exceptions to this can be a costly mistake in the long-run, as it can undermine the social fabric of a company and its ability to execute while effectively moving forward.

Looking at Strategy Execution from a 'strategy department' point of view, what is the most important topic for you?

The strategy department doesn't own the strategy. The CEO does. The role of the corporate strategy team is to inform the executive team in defining what the key strategic priorities could or should be, and how to make sure that the organisation is set up to execute most effectively against these priorities. This is our number one goal.

In addition to the typical roles of a strategy department in helping set the strategy – market research, risk/opportunity assessment, scenario-planning – it is also critical to stay close to the operations to truly understand our capabilities, execution challenges and support and encourage change agents to stretch our strategic execution abilities and fight off the status quo.

PERFORMANCE TAKEAWAYS

- Initiative management is the point where organisational performance meets individual performance, where people are added to the equation, where your strategy is translated into practice or remains on paper forever.
- Initiative management is the most important step when it comes to aligning organisational and individual performance.
- Improve initiative management in your organisation, division or team. Identify the five fundamentals, select one or more of the proven tips provided and get to work.
  1. Collect, select and prioritise the right initiatives.
  2. Optimise your resource allocation and planning.
  3. Develop your project managers.
  4. World-class project and programme management.
  5. Manage your strategic initiative portfolio.
- Don't forget to secure the outcome of your initiative management exercise. Make a solid link with the individual objectives and keep the strategy cascade flowing.

And the answer is? 'How to eat an elephant with 5 people'.
I don't remember exactly where I first saw this phrase. It was some time ago. But it struck home. Why? Because I believe this is a great metaphor. (Animal lovers and vegetarians might not like the story but hey, we are not actually eating the elephant. It's just a metaphor).

Here's how it is used.

You finalised your strategy and prepared for implementation. But the task you now face looks gigantic. It's your elephant that needs to be eaten. But if you look closely, you can break up your strategy over and over again into smaller pieces until they are easily executable. So going back to the metaphor, 'How do you eat an elephant with 5 people?'. You cut him into small pieces, be persistent and you will get there in the end.

The persistence part is particularly important but often forgotten. Good initiative management requires a large dose of persistence. In fact, that applies to Strategy Execution in general.

Before you move to the next chapter, give the following quote some thought:

"Persistence is what makes the impossible possible, the possible likely, and the likely definite"
– Robert Half

CHAPTER VIII

Challenge 6: Develop: Dice with 6 dots on each side

"An organisation's ability to learn, and translate that learning into action rapidly, is the ultimate competitive advantage"
– Jack Welch

"We now accept the fact that learning is a lifelong process of keeping abreast of change. And the most pressing task is to teach people how to learn"
– Peter Drucker

"Leadership, like swimming, cannot be learned by reading about it"
– Henry Mintzberg

O scar, a lazy CEO, sits behind his computer in his office on the third floor of a large building. While all his colleagues are working hard to earn a living, he jealously thinks about Marie, the CEO of a competing firm, who received glowing praise in local and national newspapers last week after the launch of their new product.

After a few minutes, he's quite annoyed and decides to call his secretary for his fifth coffee of the afternoon. But at that point, the 'organisational competence' fairy suddenly appears at his desk and says: *"Dear Oscar, it's your lucky day. You can wish for three competences"*. In the spur of the moment, he replies: *"I want our company to have all the competences to build the same incredible product that Marie presented at her roadshow last week"*. And so it happens. A few months later, Oscar launches his copycat product and becomes the star of the industry.

When the time comes to decide on his second competence, he reflects on it more thoroughly as he realises, by coincidence, that his Research and Development department could have developed the product without any help from the fairy. His organisation has mastered the basic competence ingredients for several years and could have been the first to market. But nobody – and certainly not Oscar himself – had ever given it much thought.

So after some serious thinking, Oscar says to the competence fairy: *"I want everyone to talk about our great brand"*. And so it happens again. And during the course of the next year, the company receives several brand recognition awards and Oscar is featured on the cover of *Business Week* and interviewed by other leading magazines desperate to discover the secrets of his brand-building success.

And then, one Friday afternoon, his Chairman unexpectedly walks into his office. *"Oscar, I've seen great things from you over the last year and I would like to offer you an opportunity. Would you be interested in becoming the new board member in our holding company?"*. Oscar, recovering from the surprise, replies: *"Well, yes, of course"* without further thought.

That night he struggles to sleep as he cannot decide how to best use his third and final free competence. If he uses it now, he loses the chance to use the competence builder for future, even bigger, challenges. Oscar postpones the decision and, for the first time in his career, decides his company needs to start investing in competence development.

After a rocky start, the company gets used to skills building and becomes quite good at it. In fact, it turns out that it already had quite a few unique capabilities that were excellent stepping stones for new products and better distribution.

And lazy Oscar?

Well, he still envies Marie from time to time and continues to drink too much coffee. But competence development remains high on his agenda, and as a result, his company moved from industry laggards to the middle of the pack. And to this day, he still has his third unused wish.

Let's leave Oscar and his company for now and get started with the final chapter of this book.

As you have probably already figured out, Chapter 8 is all about successful skills development. Being able to do what your competitors can't, demands a unique set of capabilities. But these skills don't just grow on trees or arrive courtesy of the incredible 'competence fairy'. They demand:

- *Tough choices*: you can't be good at everything.
- *Long-term commitment:* it doesn't happen overnight.
- *Motivated people:* learning new skills demands effort and a change of behaviour.

This chapter helps you to build upon the fundamentals of a successful development platform, the starting point to any successful skills development.

Some facts and figures about skills development

- Too many companies spend too much time – and money – on assessing skills. As a rule, you should invest 15 percent on skills assessment and 85 percent on skills development.
- Founded by Harvard Professor David McClelland and popularised by Daniel Goleman, competency management has had a big – both positive and negative – influence on management development. On the positive side, management development made a big leap forwards by making behaviour measurable. However, although competences made it easier to touch behaviour, many companies went over board. This meant that the competences became more important than the goal itself, to the extent that many companies lost – and still lose – themselves in competence categorisation exercises.

- The Research Institute of America found that 33 minutes after the end of a lecture, students usually retained only 58 percent of the material covered, by the second day 33 percent is retained, and after three weeks, only 15 percent. Reinforcing knowledge acquisition is clearly a critical step in the employee development process. Trained skills decay over time so you need to find ways for people to apply what they learn immediately – or provide the means to refresh what they have learnt.
- Most companies spend an average of four percent of all payroll costs on training. Best-in-class companies provide – and demand – between 50 and 100 hours per year development participation per individual and require development before or after promotions as part of a structured career path approach.
- Informal on-the-job instruction is three-to-six times more effective than formal training. Comparing the effectiveness of training and development delivered in the classroom to video technology, revealed that although both groups of trainees scored the same on learning outcomes, the conventional classroom training took 7.5 hours versus 2.6 hours for the video (Wilson, 1991).

The eight most common management development mistakes

The potential for making mistakes in the skills development arena is high. Ultimately, an organisation is aiming to develop the skills of its individuals to outclass its competitors. But the road to get there is long, bumpy and full of curves.

Here are the eight most common mistakes made by an organisation. You can also download the test if you want to evaluate the development maturity in your organisation.

 Performance download 22. Score your management development mistakes – self-assessment.

Mistake 1: No company-wide view on skills development
Most companies offer their employees some type of development oppor-tunities – whether it is *ad hoc* training, on-the-job coaching or a combina-tion of both. Few, however, use a structured, long-term approach.

The result?

No systematic company-wide skills upgrade, frustrated individuals and wasted money.

Let me give you an example. The development subject: individual objective setting. A junior manager receives objective-setting skills train-ing using Model X as part of her introduction programme. When she becomes a middle manager, the variable remuneration policy and the way objectives are set both change. As part of her new training, she has to learn other techniques – and to forget the old ones! She continues to climb the corporate ladder and becomes a senior manager. At the senior level, the corporate system kicks in. You get the problem, right?

Mistake 2: Too much at once
It can take some time before an organisation's leadership team becomes fully aware of the potential of a good Strategy Execution process. But once this potential is discovered, everything – including the skills en-hancement – needs to happen immediately for the organisation to catch up on lost time.

This seldom works well. These time-pressured programmes try to cover too much in an unrealistic time frame.

Mistake 3: Assumed that senior managers meet the skills standard
Senior managers will rarely admit that their Strategy Execution skills don't make the grade. Our business culture carries with it the automatic assumption that all managers, particularly senior managers, have great strategic thinking, coaching and budgeting skills. Questioning their skills level is usually taboo.

Mistake 4: Successful development isn't clearly understood
'Why not run a two-day classroom training programme for all our managers?'.

Heard this question before?

Probably. And you will probably agree that while the question clearly indicates a positive attitude towards development, it shows a lack of insight into what successful development actually entails.

Make sure that the launch of a training initiative doesn't give you a false sense of success. 'We organised training for everyone so that they have all the skills they need and can apply them the way we like it' is a short-sighted and potentially dangerous statement by someone who doesn't understand the dynamics of professional skills development.

Mistake 5: Training starts before the process is clear

You clearly identified the skills development need and held several training sessions. But they were a disaster.

How is that possible?

Skills training cannot start properly when managers have too many questions about the Strategy Execution process itself. Participants get frustrated when answers lack clarity or seem inadequate. And these participants will surely vent their frustrations onto future participants. In turn, some will withdraw and those who do attend will remain very sceptical and not ready for a learning experience.

Mistake 6: All effort goes into the development of a few skills

A real performance hero – someone who masters Strategy Execution – is like a triathlete. S/he might prefer one discipline but masters all three. You don't become a performance hero by excelling in only a few Strategy Execution activities, such as scorecard building or performance coaching.

Many, however, don't realise this and focus much of their energy on the activities that they have a particular aptitude for and in which they therefore feel confident.

Mistake 7: Too expensive

Senior executives who want to emphasise the importance of development and leadership, tend to show their commitment by providing budget. The result: new programmes and tools are randomly added. Everyone is focused on finding ways to spend the extra money but no one is challenging what already exists. And that's a waste of money.

Mistake 8: Average quality trainers and coaches

When companies take a cost conscious approach, it's almost always done with a short-term, one-track mind – to find trainers and coaches with a lower daily fee. In other words, they compromise on the quality of delivery to save money.

Other more effective ways to manage costs, as you will learn later on in this chapter, are ignored.

> *"Developing people in a classroom is a cost. It becomes an investment when they start applying what they learnt on-the-job. It only becomes a success the moment it has a positive impact on what the job actually needs to achieve"*

Thirty-seven tips organised according to six management development fundamentals

So by now, you know what not to do and you may be asking yourself 'What's the alternative?'.

Your keys to successful development are to build consistent, long-term and solid foundations. It's a marathon, not a sprint.

If you want your development to be on top form, exercise the following six fundamentals, the foundations of any professional management development platform.

1. Define the skills you want and how you are going to get them.
2. Manage your development portfolio.
3. Design world-class learning interventions.
4. Execute flawlessly.
5. Set development objectives.
6. Measure success.

The following tip overview will help kick-start your evaluation of the potential improvements of each guideline and define their importance during the next six months. Four-to-six months after that period, you could repeat the exercise to evaluate progress and define future actions.

 Performance download 23. Create a solid development platform – a checklist.

You can also turn the scoring exercise into an interesting team workshop.

 Performance download 24. Create a solid development platform – workshop format.

Fundamental 1: Define the skills you want and how you are going to get them

You defined your high-level strategy. Your next step is to concretise the capabilities you need to win the competitive battle within your industry. And then define a long-term development plan to achieve them.

Tip 1: Link development and strategy. I often see a disconnection between the strategy exercise on one hand and management development on the other. I hear senior management talk (a lot) about leadership development and they often do spend quite a lot of money on corporate training courses. But they don't actively work on connecting development with strategy.

Be different. Make sure your strategy drives your development actions and not the latest market trends, individual preferences or even job requirements. Or worded differently: anchor all your development into your strategy. Don't let them drift.

Tip 2: Think ahead. Developing new skills takes time – usually much more than you expect as you aim for excellence. Therefore, you need to identify today the skills you will need in three year's time. Download the workshop format to help you with this crucial exercise.

Tip 3: Let go of your old skills. While your strategy demands the development of new skills, it also requires skill divestments. Some part of your company's current skill set will become redundant or less important in supporting or acquiring competitive advantage.

Act on these competences either by outsourcing or via the reallocation of resources. Take action to redeploy... and be honest about it.

Don't put your head in the sand hoping it will go away – because it won't. People need the chance and enough time to reorient themselves. So don't hang onto your old skills and look for possible solutions early in the game.

Tip 4: Keep the right flight level. When you run a competency exercise, it's easy to drown in too much detail. You know what I'm talking about – those mapping exercises with over 150 competences.

Focus instead on those competences that will make or break your competitive position. Once you've discussed those competences (two-to-four in number), identify the key roles that will be most affected. Finally, look at it from a management perspective and the impact on how it is managed at different levels of the organisation.

Tip 5: Discuss content AND process. Don't limit your discussion exclusively to content. Make sure you also discuss *how* those crucial capabilities will be developed.

Tip 6: Involve development executives in the strategic planning process. It will help you perform better on Tip 5. Ask your executives to prepare an up-to-date review into where your company stands today in terms of skills.

Tip 7: Create excitement. You need to promote those new skills that people will need to develop over the next few years. Prepare a solid explanation as to why managers need the skills and identify the actions that the organisation can take to promote their development.

Fundamental 2: Manage your development portfolio

Your development portfolio is the collection of all your development initiatives and should be managed like any other portfolio. The training programmes, coaching, formal on-the-job training and internships, all need to fit seamlessly together to create a combination that manages to close the skills gap.

Manage your portfolio well to avoid duplication. This avoids costs and confusion. Here are some tips:

Tip 8: Make the CEO a member of the Learning Advisory Board. Such as at Motorola. If you don't have an advisory board to guide learning in your organisation, consider creating one. It needn't be too formal or heavy; a quarterly meeting will do just fine. The important part is to discuss development on a company-wide scale, across departments, with the big boss in the room.

Tip 9: Review and update overall development goals and processes. Review your company-wide development goals and processes regularly – at least once a year. The best time would be after a strategic review and before the start of the strategy cascade.

If there is a big strategy shift, there should be a long list of changes. If the list remains short, they probably haven't done their homework.

Tip 10: Develop an impact map. Don't stop once you've connected the overall development goals with your strategy. Make sure all learning intervention can also be tracked back to the overall strategy. It's a great way to challenge the need for a certain programme and, once confirmed, a great way to communicate that programme.

Here are the four questions you need to answer for each learning intervention:

1. What skills, knowledge and attitude will participants adopt?

2. How will they transfer these to their jobs?

3. With what results?

4. To what strategic goal does this contribute?

Tip 11: Use zero-based budgeting. You can reduce your overall development budget by 15 percent AND increase quality at the same time. Sounds pretty interesting, right?

Most companies manage their development budget as a closed envelope discussed once a year during the budget review. The budget owners, often HR together with line managers, are measured according to whether they stay within the global budget or not.

There is, however, a much better way. Review the effectiveness and efficiency of each programme. Define a few simple metrics and make a ranking of all your programmes each year. And say goodbye to those at the bottom on the list.

Tip 12: Use your leadership and competence dictionary correctly. A dictionary categorises and describes behaviour. This document can be very can be very valuable – but you need to be careful. Here are three things to watch out for:

- *Don't spend too much time developing one.* Don't let a consultant convince you that it would be worth developing your own dictionary from scratch. It's a waste.

  Save yourself the time and money and use a tried and tested framework. With some fine-tuning, your dictionary should be ready within a week. You can download an example from the *Strategy Execution Heroes* website.

- *Stick to it.* Once you have decided on a dictionary, make sure you stick to it. As often happens, you don't want several in circulation.

- *Don't try to teach the dictionary to everyone.* A competency dictionary offers great value for recruiters and training designers. The added value for managers however is limited as it is often too technical and not directly beneficial to their jobs. I suggest you offer it to interested managers as a nice to have, but little more.

Performance download 26. High-quality competency dictionary – an example.

Tip 13: Ensure integration with other HR processes. As well as a strong link between development and strategy, management development needs to interact with other human resource processes such as talent management, career counselling, assessment and recruitment.

Tip 14: Keep up-to-date. This is a rapidly evolving area with a constant flow of new developments to keep up with. There will be opportunities on the learning *and* the technology side. Make sure you are equipped with the knowledge to separate the good from the bad.

Fundamental 3: Design world-class learning interventions

You know which skills you want to develop. They fit into both your strategy and your global development portfolio. Now it's time to design, or 'engineer', the actual learning intervention.

In short, it's time to define who is going to learn what and in what way.

Tip 15: Adapt your approach to the needs of your target group. Even if you want to teach everyone the same thing, don't assume that the same teaching approach is the best. For example, a two-day programme for junior executives can be summarised into a two-hour session for senior executives. Same content, different delivery, better results.

Tip 16: Involve your stakeholders while developing the programme. This is a great way to fine-tune your learning approach, promote your programme and create commitment. You can use different techniques ranging from interviews, questionnaires, workshops or even seminars to test content.

Tip 17: Take the learners' points-of-view: provide relevance and context. Participants are likely to suffer from information overload in the form of classroom training, intranet, video, product documentation, job aids, online courses, how-to guides and so on.

So it's not enough to build a great training course or have an easy-to-use learning management system. Your need to offer individuals a relevant learning experience.

This requires a focus on information architecture, not just ease of use. And so you will also need to consider how the learner will track, use and apply the content.

Tip 18: Limit classroom time. It's expensive and the effects are limited. Make sure you mix/combine it with other methods such as coaching, on-the-job learning and informal learning communities.

If you do take the classroom approach, try to make the experience as interactive and useful as possible by including best-practice sharing, practical exercises and open discussions.

For most of the master classes I teach, for example, I organise an hour-long lecture two weeks in advance for the whole group (using video conference if locations are dispersed), and provide additional information on the intranet. Combined with individual telephone coaching for those who want, it reduces classroom time by 65 percent.

 Performance tip. Employ an *action learning approach*. Put managers from different disciplines in a team. Provide them with an actual business problem that keeps the company's senior management awake at night. Give them three months and some support from external facilitators and/or academics to develop a solution.

I'm a big fan of this approach as it offers many benefits. The 'student managers' discover other areas of expertise, develop new skills, learn to work effectively with colleagues, find the necessary information within the organisation, take decisions and gain senior management exposure.

Tip 19: Facilitate informal learning. In today's environment, informal learning can flourish. People can access and share information via blogs, wikis, video, rapid e-learning tools, RSS feeds, Twitter and other social networking sites. Use them wisely and they will transform any formal teaching environment into a modern informal learning experience.

Tip 20: The learning ladder. Learning is like climbing a ladder; taking one step at a time, each time building on the previous one. The four steps of the learning ladder are:
- Step 1. Acquire the knowledge.
- Step 2. Applying the knowledge to obtain better results.
- Step 3. Build expertise by regular practice.
- Step 4. Teach and coach others.

Tip 21: Manage your content on a global scale. Look beyond the programme you are engineering. Take a company-wide view. Here are six concrete suggestions:
- *Use existing content as the foundations and build on those foundations.*
- *Limit the number of models.* Avoid the temptation to add a new one each time you launch a new programme.
- *Organise a clean up.* Do an inventory. Categorise your models according to these three categories: 'essentials', 'nice to haves', 'not to haves' and take action accordingly.
- *Steal with pride.* If you don't have it, look elsewhere. Don't reinvent the wheel just for the sake of it.
- *Use the same models and techniques on all hierarchical levels.*
- *Use the same vocabulary.* Make a list, validate it and most importantly, stick to it.

Tip 22: Start early. While it takes time to develop a new skill on a company-wide scale, it also requires a significant amount of time to develop a high-quality learning experience. This makes your total timeline even longer. Start as early as possible to engineer a new learning intervention.

Fundamental 4: Execute flawlessly

The fourth fundamental is the actual learning intervention. It's all about producing effective learning outcomes and includes possible pilots, the première, the roll-out and all related activities. Here are some tips:

Tip 23: Don't start to train skills before the process is understood. If your managers don't understand the process, it will be very difficult to teach them how to successfully operate that process, even with the best skills training in the world. Let me clarify with an example: if you plan to teach managers how to use a Balanced Scorecard, make sure you first communicate how the BSC is, or will be used.

Tip 24: Always test. Make sure you test everything before you implement. Run several pilots. This isn't the time to get complacent. You can't predict the outcome of a learning experience in the engineering phase, even with the best preparation in the world. Therefore, you should always organise a dry run. And even if you had one successful dry run, you might want to consider repeating the process with a different target group or setting.

Tip 25: Motivate individuals to take responsibility for their own development. You can't force someone to learn – it's their responsibility. Communicate and institutionalise the fact that it is the individual manager's responsibility to seek out and capitalise on development opportunities.

Tip 26: Inform their managers. Familiarise participants' managers via written or video reports summarising the content of direct reports' development and ask for suggestions to reinforce learning.

Tip 27: Involve managers in the programme delivery. Although this might not be possible or desirable for all programmes, it's probably worthwhile checking for opportunities. Other organisations found the following useful:
- Whenever executive committee members are close to your development campus, invite them to teach. It works for Procter & Gamble.

- Use line managers as the primary deliverers of development as Target does.
- Consider a top-down roll-out such as that institutionalised by Xerox. That way, everybody receives the development twice, once as a trainee and once as a trainer to his/her direct reports or peers.

*Tip 28: **Watch out for scope creep.*** Trainers tend to use their last training experiences as reference, adapting those that follow accordingly. If a certain model or exercise worked well, it will probably be highlighted in the next session. When working with different trainers and after an extensive roll-out, your final sessions might be unrecognisable to those at the beginning.

*Tip 29: **Debrief regularly.*** With every training or coaching, the experience increases. Make sure all trainers and coaches share these experiences. Decide together if the programme is going to be adapted according to these learnings or not. Once decided, everyone has to stick to it.

*Tip 30: **Quality versus quantity.*** All too often, companies choose trainers or coaches based on their daily rates instead of their performance. But good trainers and coaches are hard to find. Don't compromise on delivery quality; it will cost you much more than the money you save.

If you do run into budget problems, reduce the classroom time instead.

Fundamental 5: Set development objectives

This fundamental is about anchoring your development initiatives by tying them into the individual objectives. It's a great way to improve development performance. For more information of the benefits and how to do it, see Chapter 3. In summary, here are four crucial elements:

*Tip 31: **Each individual should have development objectives.*** A simple but effective way to boost individual development efforts.

Tip 32: Provide a framework for development objectives. Most people find it difficult to express their development objectives. Make sure you provide a 'how to' with examples.

Tip 33: No skills development, no career move. This approach is very popular in consulting organisations. If you don't demonstrate that you have mastered a certain skill, you won't progress. It's very effective, but the evaluation should be carried out by more than one individual to keep the process fair.

Tip 34: Choose the right objectives for the L&D department. The Human Resources department – and more specifically the Learning and Development department – will play a leading role in transforming the development vision into reality. Make sure the right objectives are in place. Build a solid annual business plan and organise quarterly reviews with the leadership team.

Fundamental 6: Measure success

Measure the success of a development programme, define the current capability level of the organisation, determine the individual skill levels, provide self-assessment instruments… it's a world unto itself. Here are three things to watch out for:

Tip 35: Be careful with ROI. You won't be surprised if I tell you that you should evaluate the success of your development efforts. But I might surprise you by saying that the ROI (Return on Investment) approach might not be the way to do it. Yes, it sounds great and it might seem strange to go against the hype, but while many providers promise the holy grail of ROI measurement, up until now I haven't seen one that delivered on that promise. If you have, please let me know.

I would suggest spending the necessary time BEFORE your development programme starts, evaluating the need, importance, added value and cost. This way you make your investment count.

Tip 36: Avoid analysis paralysis. Don't make 'analysing' the core of your project, whether it's about identifying talents, selecting the right people, or assessing the current individual skills level. You can get side-tracked very quickly. Remember: analysis is important but it needs to serve the overall goal.

*Tip 37: **Don't go overboard on the IT side.*** I don't have to tell you that there's a lot of software available today, including that which helps with development measurement. But it's very easy to exaggerate. I've seen several companies where the automation part became the focus for the Strategy Execution process. IT can help with certain elements of the process, but ultimately, Strategy Execution remains a people-driven process.

Don't forget your Strategy Execution process owners

As you know, Strategy Execution is a widespread process where ownership is scattered across departments. In each of these departments, there are individuals with a Strategy Execution process responsibility. Their roles range from programme manager, learning and development officer to budget planner or analyst.

And they all play a crucial role in achieving a successful Strategy Execution process. So if you plan to give you managers a development boost as part of Strategy Execution, make sure you include the organisers.

But participation in the managers' programme is not enough. The Strategy Execution organisers need a deeper Strategy Execution knowledge.

To give you an idea of their development needs, I've added an excerpt from the Strategy Execution master class I teach. You can download a detailed version.

Some of the key topics are:
– Individual and organisational performance and the link between both.
– The Strategy Execution role of a manager and the challenges s/he faces.
– Best-practice building blocks of a sound Strategy Execution process.

 Performance download 27. A Strategy Execution master class – agenda.

A view on Strategy Execution by Hervé Borensztejn, Senior Vice President Human Resources, EADS

What do you consider to be the most important Strategy Execution challenge for an executive team?

I see four major strategy implementation challenges for a top team.

The first challenge

The first and probably the biggest challenge, especially in an economical downturn, is to balance the short-term pressure with the long-term ambition. Or in other words: managing different timescales. Don't forget that when companies in certain industries take a decision, they are stuck with the consequences for the next 10-to-20 years.

And senior executives don't only face this challenge for themselves. They also have to help managers across the entire organisation to balance short-term pressure with the long-term ambition. The support should, in my view, include at least the following three elements:

1. Make the timing contradiction visible in the organisation. Be explicit about the challenge. This awareness will help managers to take a short- and long-term perspective the next time they have to take a difficult decision. It helps to integrate the timing challenge into their decision-making process. It doesn't take away the tension, but improves the quality and balance of decisions between short- and long-term priorities.
2. Make sure that divisions, departments and individuals have both short- and long-term objectives.
3. Reward long-term performance. Don't just offer stock options or shares as a reward. Link long-term reward with clear, long-term threshold objectives.

The second challenge

A top team needs to take into account, and allow for, cultural differences. Provide clear, unambiguous objectives but with the freedom to define the activities most suitable to the local situation.

The third challenge

When you have a new strategy, you need to make sure it gets delivered. And your programme managers should be your FedEx delivery service. So the third execution challenge for an executive team is to build a best-in-class programme management approach with top-notch programme managers. Programme management should be part of the DNA of any organisation taking the implementation of their strategy seriously. But as with other competences, it doesn't happen overnight. You need to invest in the long-term. Here are some tips to help you get there:

- Develop a long-term plan to get the right quality and quantity of programme managers for the next 10-to-15 years.
- Rotate people between a regular job and a programme assignment.
- Set up the role of the programme manager as a fully fledged career path within the organisation.
- Build communities of practices.
- Rotate your programme managers between different types of projects to boost learning.
- Use a mentoring programme whereby senior programme managers guide the juniors and help them to develop.
- Create an attractiveness wave to let the good people know that the programme manager's role within the organisation is a key function.

The fourth challenge

To continuously improve the implementation process itself. That's the fourth execution challenge. And the two key improvement areas I see for many organisations are to simplify the process and communication. Let me explain both.

The current IT systems allows for the automation of almost everything. But this removes the need to streamline a process, often resulting in unnecessary complex activities. A company should not forget to make the performance management process as simple as possible. You should be able to explain it on one sheet of paper.

An organisation should also communicate the rationale behind the

Strategy Execution activities. The organisation should focus on the 'why' as well as the 'what'. This will help managers understand the importance of the process and turn them into players and not just puppets acting on the orders of others.

What Strategy Execution advice would you give to an ambitious manager?

Here are a few tips:

- Always ask yourself the following three questions: 'Why do I do what I do?', 'How should I do it?' and 'What should I do?'.
- Never lose sight of the big picture, resist the temptation to micro manage.
- Challenge the consensus. Don't be happy with the status quo.
- Find a mentor.
- Build a network of peers in the organisation to help you execute the strategy. Don't wait until you actually need them.

Based on your experience, what's a classic Strategy Execution mistake?

A common implementation mistake that organisations make is to forget to manage the interfaces between functions. Within a certain domain, division or department, the chain of command and control helps to get the strategy cascaded. But when implementation activities involve several silos, as they often do, the chain of command and therefore also decision processes, become blurred, resulting in implementation delays and even failure. To summarise: an implementation activity or process that runs smoothly within one department, performs less successfully across two or more departments.

Furthermore, I would also like to point out that different departments often have different motivation levels to get certain things done. A programme that is supported fully by the sales department can have a tough time getting support from the marketing department. This creates extra friction.

Looking at Strategy Execution from a 'human resources department' point of view, what is the most important topic for you?

To have an open and ongoing communication line with the other Strategy Execution process owners: the strategy and finance department. It is a crucial countermeasure against the interdepartmental problems that often occur as I described earlier.

PERFORMANCE TAKEAWAYS

- Having the competitive advantage demands a unique set of capabilities. And these skills don't just grow on trees. They demand choices, long-term commitment and motivated people.
- Building such capabilities demands a solid development approach.
- Start professionalising your development by avoiding the eight most common/classic development mistakes.
- Build a solid development platform, including the following six fundamentals:
    1. Define the skills you want and how you are going to get them.
    2. Manage your development portfolio.
    3. Design world-class learning interventions.
    4. Execute flawlessly.
    5. Set development objectives.
    6. Measure success.
- Your Strategy Execution process owners are a specific target group who deserve special attention.

And the answer is? 'A dice with 6 dots on each side'.
You cannot lose if you invest wisely in skills development. To achieve and maintain the competitive advantage requires a unique skill set that won't happen overnight or by chance.

By moving beyond the 'we need a training' approach to a best-in-class development platform, you and your organisation cannot lose.

CHAPTER IX

Challenge 7: Cascade: 1000, 999, 998… take off (it can take some time)

"In a 4x100-metre relay race, one runner starts before the other, but in the end it's the sum of the four runners that determines performance"

"There is nothing so useless as doing efficiently that which should not be done at all"
— Peter Drucker

"What's the use of measuring speed if you don't go in the right direction"

In 1996, the Summer Olympics took place in Atlanta, Georgia. Many sporting icons were pushing the limits, including Carl Lewis who won his fourth gold medal in the long jump and the amazing Michael Johnson with a new 200-metres world record.

But for me, the most memorable sports event was the men's 4x400m relay race – not so much for who crossed the finish line first, but for everything that happened before the starting gun.

The drama started the evening before when the heavily favoured American team lost the 4x100m relay to the Canadian team, pushed forward by the 'world's fastest man', Donovan Bailey. The result was particularly shocking given that the US team had never finished without a gold medal in the 4x100m relay event in any Olympic Games in which they had participated. And losing on home soil made the loss even harder to bear. But the Games were not over and the US still had a great opportunity to fight back. The next night, it was time for the 4x400m. But world-record holder Michael Johnson, the fastest man on earth for that distance, wasn't at the start line.

For the casual viewer of relay races like myself, it was hard to understand why the Americans would not want the fastest 400m runner in the world in the team. But any professional runner knows that while running is usually an individual sport, in a relay race, teamwork is the real key to winning or losing. Despite the fact that much of the time is spent with a single runner carrying the baton over his leg of the track, it is the pass-off of the batons that usually determines the outcome. Much can go wrong in a relay; the baton can be dropped or if you pass the baton too late (outside of the hand-off zone), the team is disqualified. If you pass the baton too early, the team loses the momentum of the current runner. The American team excluded Michael Johnson, not because of his running skills, but because of his lack of practice with the team in baton hand-offs. They were very aware that it is not the strength of the individual runners that decides the outcome of a relay race, rather the execution of the hand-offs. The US team went on to win the 4x400m relay that night. After the victory, I saw a TV interview explaining the tactics behind the race. My initial 'frustration' turned into respect for the decision to put the team's success first.

For me, that race epitomises the concept that the team is more important than the speed or strength of individuals. It was an important lesson for me on the importance of teamwork in realising execution success. And I have been using the story ever since to reinforce the importance of a team approach to execution. It became (unfortunately) an even better story after the double drop at the Beijing Games.

This chapter helps you approach StrategyExecution as a team sport. It covers what the *Harvard Business Review* called *"one of most influential management ideas of the past 75 years"*, the Balanced Scorecard. I won't focus on the technical aspects of the Scorecard itself since many great books have already been written on the subject. Instead, I will focus on the Scorecard execution challenges that every leader will face.

Please note that the terms 'BSC', 'Scorecard' and 'Balanced Scorecard' are used interchangeably throughout the chapter.

Some facts and figures about the Balanced Scorecard

- Contrary to popular belief, the first Balanced Scorecard was not created by Dr Robert S. Kaplan and Dr David P. Norton, but by Art Schneiderman – a fact that I was unaware of until a few years ago. At the time of its conception, Schneiderman worked as an independent consultant for Analog Devices, a mid-sized semi-conductor company. Here's the story. In 1990, Schneiderman took part in a research study by Robert Kaplan of the Harvard Business School and US management consultancy Nolan-Norton. Subsequently, Kaplan and Norton included anonymous details of this use of the Balanced Scorecard in their 1992 article on the BSC. Their article *Measures That Drive Performance* published in the *Harvard Business Review* (1992) wasn't the only paper published on the topic that year, but it was a great success and received much attention. In 1996, they published the bestselling *The Balanced Scorecard, Translating Strategy into Action*. The initial high-profile articles and this highly successful book have made the BSC well-known, but perhaps also wrongly led to Kaplan and Norton being seen as the creators of the Balanced Scorecard concept. So if you are a Scorecard fan, give credit to Robert Kaplan and David Norton, the founding fathers of modern Strategy Execution thinking, for making it common knowledge. But thank Art Schneiderman for conceptualising the Balanced Scorecard itself.
- While the term and the concept of the Balanced Scorecard was

invented by Art Schneiderman and made famous by Kaplan and Norton, the roots of performance management as an activity go further back in time. Management historian Alfred Chandler points out that early performance management practices go right back to the early 19th century and the emergence of complex organisations.

- Today, the Balanced Scorecard is considered an indispensable instrument for clarifying, communicating and managing strategy across organisations. According to research by Bain in 2010, the Balanced Scorecard is the sixth most used management instrument in today's organisations, with around 50 percent of all 11,000 survey participants making use of it. The world of academia has also jumped on the concept. By the end of 2011, Amazon listed nearly 4,000 English-language books related to the Balanced Scorecard. Meanwhile, many people have something to say about the BSC with Google hits close to seven million.

> *Did you know that the Balanced Scorecard is the sixth most used management instrument in organisations today? It's an essential management system and a cornerstone of successful Strategy Execution*

- What does a Balanced Scorecard actually do? The Scorecard provides a framework for translating an abstract strategy into specific, concrete objectives, measures, indicators and actions. It combines a 'balanced' (cause/effect) view with a 'scoring' (measuring/tracking) view. It focuses on aligning the goals of business units, teams and individual employees with the company's overall business strategy. A great Balanced Scorecard breaks a business strategy down into specific and measurable chunks. It also keeps the long-term strategic goals visible on the radar. The ultimate goal of a Balanced Scorecard is to experience Strategy Execution as a continuous process. Today, the BSC provides much more than multi-view measurement; in many organisations, it's an essential management system and a cornerstone of successful Strategy Execution.

- By helping organisations detect problem areas and ensuring that managers and employees focus their energies in the right areas, the Balanced Scorecard also becomes an important foundation for operational management.
- The Balanced Scorecard should not be viewed as a controlling instrument. Its ultimate goal is to create focus for what's really important for the future, ensuring that all employees contribute to the realisation of the company's mission and strategic goals. Measurement is a means to reaching a goal and not a goal in itself.
- The Scorecard is also about learning and teaching; about your strategy, the assumptions you have made regarding winning in the marketplace and the value proposition you have put forward. It can be a crucial lever to communicating your strategy.
- If you look into the Balanced Scorecard, at some point you will face the automation challenge. According to 2GC research, more than 100 BSC reporting applications (supporting the automation of data collection, reporting and analysis) were available in February 2011. A previous survey revealed that, of all the companies that used BSC software, roughly one-third used office software to report their Balanced Scorecard, one-third used bespoke software developed specifically for their own use and one-third used one of the many commercial packages available.

The 4 benefits of a Balanced Scorecard

I'm an early Scorecard adopter having used it since 1996. I've learnt the hard way what works and what doesn't. One of the most important things on my experience list is that you need to decide *how* you use the BSC in your organisation. Or put differently, a Scorecard can offer you and your company a variety of benefits depending on how it is introduced and used. The crucial question is therefor not *if* you use the Scorecard but *how* you use it. For maximum return, you need to look below the surface, understand your options and make a definite choice about *'how our company should use the Scorecard for maximum benefit'*. It's like buying a smart phone and using it only for phone calls. You'll miss out on all the other great benefits that such a phone can offer.

To better understand this crucial point, let's take a short journey back in time. The first article in the *Harvard Business Review* in 1992 about the Scorecard was called *Balanced Scorecard – Measures That Drive Performance*. As you can see from the title, the concept of the Scorecard was initially designed to help companies measure performance differently – by focusing on more than financial indicators alone. (Research in the early '90s showed that 90 percent of all indicators were financial).

But what most people don't know is that soon after the publication of this first article in 1992, the basic ideas rapidly evolved and two movements were initiated. I call these the *'Upstream'* and the *'Downstream'* Balanced Scorecard movements.

Let's look at the Upstream movement first. When the early adopters started using the Scorecard for measuring, they quickly learnt that it had other more important benefits. They realised that the Scorecard also provides an interesting framework to cascade strategy. Four years after the publication of their first article, Kaplan and Norton included some of these findings in their book *The Balanced Scorecard: Translating Strategy into Action* (1996) and continued to explore the cascading idea further in their later books, particularly *The Strategy-focused Organisation – How Balanced Scorecard Companies Thrive in the New Business Environment (2000)* and *Strategy Maps: Converting Intangible Assets into Tangible Outcomes (2004)*. Others followed this same path and positioned the BSC as an ideal approach for cascading an overall strategy. It was positioned as the next logical thing for a company to do once it had finished a strategy revamp or update. The Upstream Balanced Scorecard movement was born.

The Downstream movement was initiated by the software industry that eyed automation opportunities. The software vendors smelt money and started promoting KPI automation at every opportunity. Their storyline focused on the scoring element and positioned the

Scorecard as a tracking tool – a dashboard for every manager to track his/her own performance with, if possible, an automated data upload. The Balanced Scorecard was positioned as *the* instrument to measure and visualise this measurement. Positioned as an instrument without any link with strategy, the *Downstream Balanced Scorecard* movement saw the light of day.

Both schools – Upstream and Downstream – had their share of followers, but the Downstream movement had a stronger voice fueled by underlying financial interest. So, unfortunately, in many organisations, for around a decade, Scorecard projects were mainly about building fancy, automated dashboards.

Thankfully, a lot has changed and several Balanced Scorecard automation companies have adopted a different approach and embraced the Upstream potential of a BSC. They now know that a Scorecard approach that's not embedded in their client's strategy cascading process will not survive.

With this brief history in mind, let's take a look at the four major benefits that a Balanced Scorecard can offer:

1. It breaks your strategy into smaller pieces
2. It measures strategy progress
3. It improves strategy communication, one of the weak spots of Strategy Execution
4. It develops the analytical and conceptual thinking power of individuals

If you have a state-of-the-art, optimised Scorecard, these are the four areas where you will get your return.

How well does your organisation score in terms of these four benefits? From my experience, most organisations using a BSC miss out on one or more of these and don't maximise the potential of their Scorecard.

In the next section, Balanced Scorecard expert Carlos Guevara and myself share our tips on how to increase your BSC return, but for now let's dig a little deeper into each of the four benefits.

Benefit 1. The BSC cascades your strategy

The Balanced Scorecard helps you cascade strategy. That's the most important benefit. Your strategy is your big elephant that you have to cut into pieces. The Balanced Scorecard helps you achieve this. The cause and effect relationships of Scorecards on different levels force you to make your strategy thinking more visible and facilitates debate and challenging. Have a look at the 8 again, the execution framework explained on page 21. You will find 'cascade strategy' in top right. That's where the Balanced Scorecard fits in – a methodology to cut your strategy into pieces and cascade it across the organisation. The Scorecard is a company's strategy waterfall and can either be a torrent such as the powerful Niagara Falls on the Canada-America border or the almost invisible sources that feed Iceland's hot springs.

Benefit 2. The BSC measures your strategy progress

If you ask 100 managers 'What's the use of a BSC?', 98 will include the response 'It's for measurement' within their answer. And there's nothing wrong with that, as long as it's not the only answer. And therein lies the fundamental problem with Scorecards in many organisations.

The Balanced Scorecard can measure, but that's not the only or most important thing it does or should do. It's like saying that a flat screen TV is great as a wall decoration or that a car keeps you dry when it's raining – you just miss out on the most important benefits such as watching your favourite movies and programmes in high quality or getting you from A-to-B the most convenient way possible.

There is no doubt that Scorecards improve your measuring, but by focusing on this benefit alone, you will only reap 25 percent of all four potential benefits. I see too many managers getting carried away with the measuring part and when that happens a Scorecard approach does the organisation more harm than good. Companies that lose track of the goal and let the means take over are on the wrong track. The Scorecard becomes a nice word for describing a set of measures, rather than a building block of your Strategy Execution framework.

Benefit 3. The BSC communicates your strategy

Cascading strategy is all about the collective understanding of the overall company strategy. And while this strategy can be designed by just a few people, the Strategy Execution demands effort from a much bigger crowd to succeed.

I previously described in Chapter 4 how important it is to get the strategy into the *head, heart* and *hands* of all your employees. A strategy needs to come alive at each of these three levels. The Balanced Scorecard will help you get the job done. Here's how:

Helps reach the head: A strategy is nothing but a choice (or decision, if you prefer) based on a set of underlying hypotheses fed by data. The key word here is 'underlying'. If you only give me the outcome, but I don't know or understand the underlying hypothesis you used to make your choice (or read, to reach your decision), I will probably not understand the complete picture. It's very difficult to judge the iceberg if you can only see the section above the water's surface.

> *"A Balanced Scorecard helps turn parrots – people who just repeat what they have heard – into ambassadors – people who understand the what and why and can reason decisions with others"*

Thanks to the visualisation of the cause and effect relationships within the Scorecard, underlying assumptions surface. This makes the link between *'what'* you want to achieve and *'why'* you want to achieve it much clearer. If I understand the link between the 'why' and the 'what' in your strategy story, I can become a strategy ambassador who reasons with others about the importance of a certain choice, rather than a parrot that simply repeats what it has heard.

Helps reach the heart. By building a Scorecard for your organisation, division or team, people become part of the strategy cascading process. And although many of them have the direction set out (especially at the lower levels of an organisation), people can still colour in within the overall framework. And by doing so, they will find an answer to the crucial question, 'What's in it for me?'. This happens by participating in the discussion. Phil Jones, a Balanced Scorecard expert, frames it very nicely; it is about the quality of conversation, because quality of conversation leads to better understanding and decision-making and quality of action. So the emphasis of our Scorecard work is on improving the quality of decision-making, team by team. Some of this is about having better information. Much of it is about a greater understanding of the objectives, situation, actions and behaviours.

A second advantage that the BSC offers to reach the heart is strong visual identity. People first remember form, then colour and finally, content. Offering a sexy strategy map has a strong visual recognition effect and helps to make the strategy stick – most people run faster with a nice one-pager than a 25-page brick.

Helps reach the hands. Building a high-quality Scorecard doesn't come easy. Drilling down the strategy and cascading it to a level where it becomes actionable at your level in the organisation is hard work. The cascading process forces you to think about the strategy storyline and its execution challenges. Absorbing this information and producing actionable items will get your hands dirty.

The strategy cascade does not stop with your Scorecard either. So you are challenged again (or forced to, depending on your mindset) to cut the action items into smaller chunks, transforming them into lower-level objectives, projects or individual objectives for yourself or your team members. This 'cutting' process will help you identify potential mistakes in your thinking and force you to go back, maybe even one or two levels up or sideways (the big alignment challenges are often horizontal, across silos and not so much vertical, across the hierarchical levels). So, once again, there is a lot of doing that will make the strategy story stick greater.

Benefit 4. The BSC boosts your strategic thinking skills

The fourth benefit is a Scorecard advantage that few advertise or promote. And that's a shame, as I believe it's one of the most important returns you can have.

I'm a big fan of integrating Balanced Scorecard building into the leadership track. This is especially useful in operational environments where 95 percent of the challenges that managers face are focused on finding short or medium-term solutions. There will come a time when your best managers in operational jobs move up. And they should be ready. Learning to work with the Balanced Scorecard in a leadership track is a great way to train and get those analytical and conceptual thinking muscles in shape. So the Balanced Scorecard offers the opportunity to build and stretch those strategic thinking skills, an opportunity rarely present in lower-level operational environments.

What not to do with the Balanced Scorecard

The Balanced Scorecard offers you four major benefits, but it's not the solution to all of your problems (although you might well wonder if you look at what Scorecards are used for in some organisations). The BSC has earnt its stripes – it is the best-known approach for cascading strategy – an important building block of the 8, the overall Strategy Execution framework. But the Scorecard also has its limitations.

You should see these limitations not in absolute terms, but in relative terms – as in, there are other, better ways of tackling certain building blocks of the 8 framework. It is like walking from Paris to Rome. You can do it, but there are more efficient ways to cover the distance.

Here are four activities where I would not recommend using a Scorecard:

First of all, a Balanced Scorecard *should not replace a strategy.* Some people think that having the four perspectives of the Scorecard visualised in a sexy strategy map is the same as having a strategy. Well, it's not. Just because you have a map doesn't mean that the destination is clear. A strategy map can be a great instrument to communicate your strategy, but doesn't dig deep enough into the strategic positioning questions you need to tackle. So make sure you have a strategy before you start.

> *"Don't fool yourself: having a strategy map is not the same as having a strategy"*

Secondly, a Balanced Scorecard *should not be used to manage individual objective setting*. I have seen some companies go all the way, using Scorecards to define and monitor individual objectives, but with little success. Very quickly, the instrument becomes the centre of attention rather than the individual's performance.

Thirdly, a Scorecard *should not replace operational measurement*. There are many aspects of your business that you should need and want to keep track of. But not all those measures need to be in the BSC. Sometimes I feel that the Scorecard has become an accountant's instrument. And that's not the objective, is it?

Finally, a Balanced Scorecard should not *be used as a project or programme management instrument*. Yes, there should be initiatives in your Scorecard that are bundled into projects and/or programmes. They are an essential element of the cascade (that are unfortunately often left out), but the BSC is too static to monitor and manage them.

How to get more from your Balanced Scorecard

The first section covers tips to introduce a Balanced Scorecard into your organisation. The second section offers insights to help you achieve more from your existing Scorecard approach.

14 tips to get the basics right

You can download and prioritise tips with download 28 or organise a workshop with your team using download 29.

 Performance download 28. Introduce a Balanced Scorecard approach – a checklist.

Performance download 29. Introduce a Balanced Score-card approach – workshop format.

Tip 1: Don't rely on the first BSC book. Knowledge evolves and 1996, when the first Scorecard book was launched, is light years ago. If you start a BSC project in your organisation and see project members running around with the original Scorecard book complete with highlighted paragraphs, something is very wrong. The first Balanced Scorecard book is not the reference. New best practices have emerged so start your project with up-to-date knowledge.

Tip 2: Watch out for the Scorecard gurus. Many so-called BSC 'gurus' have jumped on the Balanced Scorecard wagon and produced a plethora of books all pretending to be the 'definitive' BSC book. Amazon lists more than 4,000 books under Balanced Scorecards. Take some time to dig into the subject. Listen to different opinions, build a broad view and make your own mind up, taking into account the specific needs of your organisation. Remember, just because something works very well in one company doesn't mean it will do the same for yours.

Tip 3: Manage the introduction of the Balanced Scorecard as a change project. The Balanced Scorecard impacts the way your managers manage – so the implementation effort will therefore demand change effort from everyone. Increase your success rate dramatically by managing your BSC introduction as a change project, rather than the introduction of an instrument.

Tip 4: Managing change requires strong leadership. There is no change without strong leadership. It's that simple.

Tip 5: Communicate process before content. Don't wait until you have the content ready – start right away by communicating the advantages, project timings, roles and responsibilities of the Balanced Scorecard. Proactive, no-nonsense communication prevents misunderstandings and creates buy-in. Take a look at some of the communication best-practices in change projects – they're quite useful.

Tip 6: Know what you want to achieve. A Balanced Scorecard can serve many purposes and offers four distinct benefits. You won't be able to reap all of them in the first year, so choose carefully. Once you make a choice, stick to it and make sure you get those benefits before focusing on something else. I like to focus on the cascading and learning part first, on the communication second, moving onto the measuring part last.

Tip 7: Define your cascading architecture. It's important to select a cascading approach upfront. You have several options to cascade objectives, measures, targets and initiatives. Your choice depends on your overall goal. For example, cascading by regions will help you empower a geographical approach, cascading by business lines will help you achieve higher autonomy and accountability for your profit centres. Cascading themes, like innovation, customer experience or green economy, will help you improve the coordination between several apparently disconnected organisational units around a particular theme.

Tip 8: Avoid the classic pitfalls. Many companies have gone through the process of introducing the Balanced Scorecard. It's a good idea to do some research to get a feeling for your organisation's particular situation. This will help avoid some of the classic pitfalls. Typical mistakes that companies have made in the past include:

- Senior management is not convinced and shows little commitment
- The Scorecards are developed by 'the happy few'
- The internal/external project members have limited or only theoretical knowledge
- The Balanced Scorecard is only used by top management
- The Balanced Scorecard stays too long at the development stage before being launched and used
- There are not enough links to the strategy and planning processes
- The content of the Balanced Scorecard is unrealistic
- The Balanced Scorecard is only used for remuneration purposes

*Tip 9: **Get your vocabulary straight**. An objective is neither a measure nor a target. A short overview of the key words and what they mean helps to avoid confusion. Choose the words that fit your organisation and make sure people stick to them. And do make sure you know what you are talking about!

*Tip 10: **What's the aim?** Your goal is not to get into the Balanced Scorecard hall of fame. Your goal is to cascade strategy to maximum effect. If that works with a dull approach that the Scorecard community doesn't find sexy, that's too bad. Your goal is to get the strategy into the heads, hearts and hands of the people in your organisation, not to stroke your ego.

*Tip 11: **Set the expectations right from the start**. Be honest with your stakeholders about timing and results. Setting up the basics may take a few weeks, but seeing real benefits will take far longer. Don't oversell yourself. Make your stakeholders aware upfront that implementing a Balanced Scorecard is a transformational journey better approached as a marathon than as a sprint.

*Tip 12: **Get your measures right**. From the start, your focus should be to cascade strategy. But, at some point, you will want to measure strategy progress. Here are a few basics to get it right:

- *Aim for relevance.* Performance indicators should be deduced from strategic objectives and measure the degree of achievement. Focus your measurement on the outcomes, not the means. Here's an example from Carlos: *"Once, in a BSC workshop, a Supply Chain Manager told me that one of her key objectives for the next year was to implement a new procurement system. She had even set out the measures and targets – in 15 months the system should 'go live'. I asked, "Why do you need a new procurement system?". After a few seconds pause, she replied: "You are right, that's not my objective, that's my initiative. My objective would be to improve the efficiency of procurement".* In this example, the real benefit, the outcome, is a more efficient procurement. And that outcome deserves a measure and one or more targets.

> *"What's the value of measuring speed if you are driving in the wrong direction?"*

- *Aim for simplicity.* Using ratios – correlating two variables such as cost per unit or CAPEX per employee – may seem like a good idea at the start, but when your ratios are so complex that you can't explain if it is going wrong because of your numerator or denominator, using ratios become useless. Measures should be simple to understand and easy to act upon.

- *Aim for recurrent measures.* Always spend enough time defining your measures. Stay away from those that can only be measured once a year. Great measures are backed up by reliable data, can be reported frequently and are easy for target setting. First of all, this means no 'yes/no' indicators. Indicators should be constantly measurable and suitable to show development over time (e.g. the improvement or deterioration of the indicator over several periods). This means that an indicator that is measuring the achievement of a certain condition, such as a quotation of the division at the stock exchange, is not a good indicator, even though the objective might show strategic relevance.

- *Aim for consistency.* Performance indicators have to be consistent over time and across several operating units. It starts with a clear indicator so that measuring the same value by two different people gives the same result and a stable measurement process. How? Make a definition card that clarifies the purpose of the measure, the source of its data elements, the calculation method, frequency of update, data owner or owners and evaluation limits. If management asks "Where did this number come from?", you probably missed a few steps.

- *Aim for a good mix between leading and lagging indicators.* A lagging indicator is an indicator that looks at the past. It trails behind reality and offers an accurate, but historical view of the facts, such as turnover. A leading indicator tries to predict the future. It shows trends before lagging indicators show the actual result, for example, customer satisfaction before customer loyalty. Your dashboard should have enough leading indicators so you can predict where you are going and take corrective action if needed. Having only lagging indicators limits your corrective ability. Also, having a dashboard full of lagging indicators gives you a false sense of control.

> *"If you have too many rear view mirrors, it will be very difficult to see the road ahead"*

- *Aim for efficiency.* If it takes you a week to collect the data or you need to reconfigure your complete ERP system to get it automated, you are probably better off selecting another measure.

Tip 13: Be careful when setting a target for a new measure. Target setting is one of the more tricky parts of developing your Balanced Scorecard, especially when you are dealing with new measures without a target baseline. Setting the right targets is about finding the optimal level of stress that you want to inject into your organisation. So take care first time round – set targets that are too conservative and you won't stretch people, set targets that are too ambitious (read unachievable) and they may be seen as a dream, discouraging action.

Tip 14: Use benchmarking with care. Benchmarking is one way to determine ambitious, yet realistic targets. But you should use this option with care and a sense of realism. I say 'realism' because you won't find solid benchmark data for all of your measures and 'with care' because you need to relate the level of the bar to your strategic choice. You don't necessarily want to be the best, so a threshold target can be your best option if you don't differentiate yourself on this aspect of the business. Here's an example: benchmarking is not a case of "Our competitors' costs for topic 'X' are 15 percent lower than ours, so we must reduce our costs by at least 15 percent", but rather "Our competitors' costs for topic 'X' are 15 percent lower than ours. They are the cost player in our industry, but we're the product leader. An appropriate threshold target (even if you are the product leader, your price elasticity is not unlimited) for us is a cost reduction of seven percent."

Beyond Kaplan and Norton: 24 tips for the advanced practitioner

The Balanced Scorecard has been around for more than 20 years. Many tips have been written on how to build the perfect Scorecard. Carlos and I have tried to go beyond the typical list of tips and provide a fresh perspective for the advanced practitioner.

To help find the tips you need, they are organised around the four BSC benefits explained earlier in this chapter. You can download and prioritise tips with download 30 or organise a workshop with your team using download 31.

 Performance download 30. Advanced Balanced Scorecard tips – a checklist.

 Performance download 30. Advanced Balanced Scorecard tips – a checklist.

I. Improve cascading quality

Tip 1: Adapt your size. The BSC should be adapted to the size of the user group. You don't need a cannon to kill a fly. Smaller units don't have – or need – the resources to handle a complex Scorecard. If you use Scorecards for large *and* small units, you need two different approaches – a basic and a more detailed way of working. If you don't, you will overshoot for the smaller units and create frustration. So adopt according to size – a bare version for the smaller units, a standard version for mid-sized teams and a full-size version for big units.

Tip 2: The BSC is not the end station... so don't stop! Strategy Execution is a continuous process. The Scorecard is one technique for cascading strategy to the next level. But cascading strategy to the next level down is just the first step in the cascading process. If you stop there, your strategy will never end up in all the hands, hearts and heads of your employees. Make sure you continue to translate the Scorecard output to a solid project and programme portfolio and that you succeed in getting the necessary actions and activities into the individual objectives of all team members.

Tip 3: Start with the right content. A well-designed Balanced Scorecard reflects your company's strategy – so make sure your strategy is clear at the start. If it isn't, take the necessary time to clarify. The quality of the strategy cascade can only be as good as the quality of the strategy it starts from. Challenge your strategy for inconsistencies and loopholes.

Tip 4: Don't let your budget process dictate your company's future. What is the most important process in an organisation? Based on the amount of attention it receives, I would say the budgeting process. In many organisations, budget is king. Many see the budgeting process as the trigger (because they are forced to do so) of a limited reflection process to identify (read justify) how much more money they will need the following year. They get into a battle with those at the top and after some struggle and cutbacks, return to business as usual. Many companies would make a big leap forwards if the strategy cascade process received the same attention as the budgeting process. Ideally, the cascading process should lead and the budget process follow. A solid strategy cascading process with the BSC is a great counterbalance for an out of control budget approach – a situation prevalent in many organisations.

> *"If companies would invest as much time in their strategy cascade as they do in their budgeting process, most would perform a lot better"*

Tip 5: 'We have a strategy map' is not the same as 'We have a strategy'. When I see a strategy map, my favourite question is *"Where's the strategy?"*. Just because you have a strategy map, doesn't mean that you have a strategy. A strategy map often looks fancy but mostly it's a lot of 'map' and very little 'strategy'. I like a written strategy document in Word format with all the hypotheses clearly explained. I like a document where there is no hiding behind an arrow and people saying 'But that's what that arrows means' when you point out something that isn't clear.

I'm not against strategy maps at all. In fact, they can be quite useful to communicate strategy and create involvement. But I've seen too many sexy PowerPoint presentations that look strategic from a distance, but are far from strategic if you take a closer look and start questioning the content. So I advocate prudence. Each strategy map should include a written two or three-page Word document that captures customer and industry insights and the choices that you have made based on this information (the Who), plus a clear overview of the way you deliver unique value to your customer (the What) using your value chain. You will find more on this topic in the next chapter.

Tip 6: Create a strong core team that involves others. Take your time selecting the people who will support the Scorecard's implementation. Make sure you have people with a good level of business understanding, excellent facilitation skills and the ability to mobilise people. Motivate the core team to involve as many people as possible through workshops to ensure enough buy-in before you move forwards. Critical mass is key to propel a transformation forward.

Tip 7: Cascade more than objectives. The cascading process provides a great opportunity to align the whole organisation towards the strategy.

Cascading your targets – clarifying how much of a specific corporate target will come from each organisational units – and your initiatives – illustrating the contribution of each unit – will help you improve alignment by tackling upfront the interdependencies that may exist across your organisation. Alignment can happen vertically – between 'parent' and 'child' organisational units – and horizontally – between 'sister' organisational units. So cascading objectives, measures and initiatives are all key to achieving horizontal and vertical alignment.

*Tip 8: **Don't rely too much on external consultants.*** Cascading strategy is a learning process. Don't miss the opportunity to capture all the knowledge that's generated during BSC implementation by over-utilising external resources. Appoint your (best) internal resources to the implementation team, especially future leaders that you would like to develop. The BSC implementation programme offers a unique window of opportunity to understand the essentials of your business and contribute to its future performance.

II. Improve measurement quality

*Tip 9: **Avoid measuring mania.*** Be careful with the slogan *'What gets measured gets done.'* Many companies lose valuable time playing around with performance measures in their organisation, debating the bells and whistles of their flashing traffic lights, measuring things because someone repeated the famous quote *'What gets measured gets done'*. I'm not against measuring, but it needs to become part of the overall execution framework and aimed at the strategy. It cannot be a stand-alone process. Think about this, *'What's the value of measuring speed if you are driving in the wrong direction?'*.

*Tip 10: **Don't believe everything that software vendors tell you.*** Measuring mania has been fuelled by software vendors – the Downstream Balanced Scorecard movement I talked about earlier in this chapter. Automation can be a good thing, but it needs to be approached with care. As I said before, good BSC software vendors no longer focus on measurement alone, but there are still quite a few of the 'old school' around who like to get the big KPI roll-out projects.

The Balanced Scorecard is the building block of the overall strategy framework – the 8. It's not a dashboard, it's part of a process. Technology is an enabler and should come once your process is stable. So make sure your system is working properly in manual mode before you introduce automation technology.

Tip 11: *Think about a measuring concept*. A great way to select the right measures is to approach the measurement challenge from a helicopter perspective – by looking for a measurement framework or concept that fits your value chain. For example, if you look at your sales process from a mile away, you are able to identify the most critical steps in the process and select the right measures to indicate progress. You won't need a measure and matching targets for every step. This has two benefits: it drastically reduces the number of measures and forces you to focus on the most crucial parts. This approach works for all building blocks of the value chain. Download 32 offers you some measuring frameworks to get you started.

Performance download 32.
Measuring frameworks – examples.

Tip 12: *Learn to visualise gaps*. 'A picture is worth a thousand words' perfectly summarises this tip. Learn to visualise your message. It will become much more powerful. But don't just use any visual. Make sure that the message and the visual reinforce each other. A great book on the topic is the classic *Say It with Charts* by Gene Zelazny.

Tip 13: *Focus on behaviours that drive performance*. Measuring the number of daily pizza deliveries by a delivery guy can lead to an improvement in delivery times to customers as much as the possibility of the delivery guy having an accident due to excessive speed. People do what they are measured for, not what they are told to. Think about the behaviours that your measures drive. What can go wrong? What kind of implicit behaviours are you incentivising?

Tip 14: Don't let your current measures define your future strategy. Imagine that you need to develop the BSC for a hotel chain that needs to move from a 'maximise occupation' strategy to a 'maximise profit per room' strategy. As you would expect, the current transactional systems are designed to measure utilisation with very little data available to monitor the profitability per room. If you would have to let the available measures define the shape of your BSC, you would end up measuring exactly what you need to change. Don't be afraid to introduce new measures in your Scorecard. It may be a good indication that you are pointing towards a change in your strategic direction and that a new strategy is emerging.

Tip 15: Fight the hockey stick syndrome. This is all about target setting, particularly when there is a link between hitting targets and financial bonuses. Watch out for people who sell a great dream – a sky-high, long-term target – to enthuse you but have a very slow, non-linear build-up. It looks much like a hockey stick if you put the targets in a two-axe visual. When a bonus is involved, always challenge the reality of the long-term goal (the one that determines the size of the bonus) and increase the ramp up towards the end goal.

III. Get more communication benefits

Tip 16: Strategy communication is much more than a good-looking PowerPoint presentation on the intranet. You communication does not end when the slides are put on the shared drive. This is just the beginning. When you are tired of the message, you have only reached three percent of your target population.

Tip 17: Develop a 'strategy story'. How many times have we heard two managers telling a slightly different strategy story, but using the same slide deck? If your strategy is not detailed, people will fill in the blanks using their imagination. If your strategy is vague, it will not survive the Scorecard cascade. The end result may look good on paper, but there will be a variety of messages running through your organisation depending on who the messenger is.

If you want your strategy to survive the cascading round, you have to do two things. Firstly, detail the message and secondly, work on the communication skills of the messenger. Put another way, develop a detailed strategy script and label this the 'official story'. Then teach your managers to repeat the storyline until everyone feels comfortable with the content.

Tip 18: Your CEO on YouTube. One of my favourite ways of achieving consistency of message is to make an 8 to 15-minute video of the CEO giving a strategy message that can be shown in sessions. I prefer an interview format as most people don't like speaking directly to the camera. We discuss the questions upfront before recording it and editing to perfection (I use a frozen image between each question allowing for easy cutting and pasting).

Exercise. Do you have strategy consistency?

Want to convince your colleagues to spend more time on strategy communication? Here's a trick that will get it done.

Get yourself a TV crew for a day. It does not have to be anything fancy – just one or two people and a video camera (an amateur camera is fine). Invite 40 people from the organisation to a designated room, giving each one a 15-minute slot. Ask each individual one question: "What are the three most important points for our company to succeed?"

The answers themselves shouldn't run to more than a few minutes, but you will need the 15 minutes to explain what you do to reassure participants. Once you have all the answers, cut and paste them into one video. Bring the senior team around the table, watch the video and have a discussion on what you have seen.

It's a great way to show inconsistencies and create a burning platform to spend more time and energy communicating the strategy. I often use this approach in combination with a short survey to get the 'engineers' on board.

A few more tips: make sure you invite a good mix of people, ranging from the CEO, a few members of the management team, people from staff and business lines and those from corporate and field. If you are dealing with various global locations, you can instruct people to interview a few people at key locations and edit the material into one video. If edited with care, the effect can be quite dramatic.

Tip 19: Use your BSC beyond those boring meetings. Don't limit the use of your Scorecard exclusively to Scorecard-related meetings. We have seen managers walking around with their Balanced Scorecards actually having created pocket versions or there are posters on the walls and other types of communication that allow employees to pull out their BSC in any discussion, whether in a meeting room or while having coffee with their colleagues.

IV. BSC as a strategic thinking booster

Tip 20: Demystify the words 'strategy' and 'innovation'. In many organisations, these two words carry an aura of complexity and mystique. Lots of people like to use them – especially strategy tourists – and even cultivate them, but most don't really know their meanings. One of the best ways to help others (and maybe yourself) is by demystifying them and push the real meanings forward. How? The next chapter on strategy will help you get this done.

Tip 21: Teach people how to debate strategy. Operational people are like firefighters – they are always ready to react at a moment's notice. But reacting to something that has already happened demands a different skill-set than debating things that have not happened. If you are not used to doing this, it can be quite a challenge. One of the first things I learned at Arthur D. Little was scenario thinking – learning to think about the future by looking at the same problem with a different set of fixed parameters each time.

The first thing you have to learn is how to translate your assumptions into parameters that you can control in a scenario exercise (it sounds harder than it is. The key question is 'Let's assume that...'). It's a very useful skill to dive deeper into different assumptions, using a common language.

A second important skill – and an often-overlooked one – is listening. As you are talking about something that has not yet happened, you have to feed the basis of your discussion on the assumptions of others. That means that you have to be able to capture them and understand them. Listening skills are highly undervalued. Interventions such as 'So you're saying that...' or 'Do I understand correctly that...' are crucial to get a solid strategy debate off the ground. Remember: the quality of a strategy debate is greatly determined by the listening skills of the participants. When you are not able to feed off other's ideas, the discussion becomes a 'convincing' contest and flatters nothing but the ego.

Tip 22: Integrate strategic thinking into your learning programme. One great way to demystify words and teach people strategic thinking skills is to offer them the opportunity to try and fail in a safe environment at an early stage of their career. I'm always surprised that most leadership programmes fail to integrate modules to teach and challenge the strategic thinking abilities of their leaders. I advocate that each leadership track should have those building blocks – and not only for the most senior people but at each level. That does not mean that you should deliver the same content or exercises at each level. You should start slowly and build it up gradually. And by the time your leaders arrive at the senior stage, they will have the background to apply what they have learnt in real life.

An MBA is not the solution. Yes, an MBA will teach you the building blocks of strategic thinking (if it's a good course), but you will never be able to send everyone on such a programme and as a result you create an atmosphere of 'strategy is for the elite'. I'm a strong believer that every manager or potential manager should get the opportunity to learn about strategy and stretch their strategic thinking skills.

Tip 23: Balanced Scorecard walk-in sessions. A Scorecard is based on a number of assumptions. The better the assumptions, the better the quality. The more assumptions are challenged, the better they get. Do you have a systematic process in your organisation to do this? Not everyone has the most conceptual boss in the world with time on his/her hands. Not everyone is willing to show that they struggle with certain parts of their thinking. So how can you solve that? I'm a big fan of Balanced Scorecard walk-in sessions. How do they work? During the Scorecard season – the period during the year when everyone is cascading the overall strategy to their working environment – you set up a room where individuals or small teams can go to debate their Scorecard. Show what they have done and get challenged. It shouldn't take long, between 30 and 60 minutes. Short discussion can change assumptions and really help people step up their game.

Tip 24: Identify conceptual thinking power. A few years ago I participated in a research programme. The goal was to identify which and to what extent leadership competencies could be developed. The conclusion was that from all 24 competencies we looked at, conceptual thinking (the helicopter view) was the competency with the least development potential. Or put another way, out of a set of 24 leadership competencies, conceptual thinking is the most difficult to develop.

So what do you do when you know that conceptual thinking power is hard to develop? You need to start as early as possible in the career to trigger conceptual power. If you start the development process when people actually need the skills in their job (after a promotion to senior level, for example), you will be too late.

Remember: if a senior team does not have enough conceptual thinking power, it will get into trouble. Many companies try to solve this by getting strategy consultants in, but if the team is unable to challenge the concepts/assumptions they propose, you won't win.

A view on Strategy Execution by Abdullah Al Nuaimi, Director General, ADWEA and Toufic Allaf, Technical Advisor and BSC Implementation Champion

The Abu Dhabi Water and Electricity Authority (ADWEA) consists of 14 government subsidised and private companies that supply electricity and potable water to the 1.4 million people of the Emirate of Abu Dhabi. One company is a single procurer and seller of electricity and water, 10 produce electricity or water, one transmits electric power and two are electric power distribution companies. ADWEA serves an area of 67,340km², almost 90 percent of the UAE's total area.

Founded in 1998 to replace the government-owned Abu Dhabi Water and Electricity Department and to privatise the water and electricity sector in Abu Dhabi, ADWEA delivered successfully on its mission. During the following decade and despite the complexities of privatisation, ADWEA succeeded in expanding power capacity and water supply beyond demand, despite its workforce decreasing by almost a third and (towards 2009) its customer base roughly doubling.

The next 20 years present as much, if not more of a challenge than that faced by the pioneers responsible for ADWEA's early development. Not only is the explosion in water and electricity demand of the past 10 years projected to continue, but there are also significant pressures to reduce reliance on government subsidies by improving efficiencies and the overall quality of service.

There has also been a growing awareness of climate change and a subsequent worldwide commitment towards more sustainable methods of production and distribution. Against this backdrop, ADWEA must ensure that it is able to meet the following challenges: firstly, to create an overarching vision and then translate it into practical actions coupled with the capabilities necessary to bring about change; secondly, to identify and quickly embed new ways of working which will bring about considerable performance improvement and thirdly, to implement 'feedback loops' to learn and develop from the outcomes of the decisions made and actions taken. This has led to the recognition that a new approach to strategy development (with clear links to performance management) is necessary.

In September 2009, ADWEA's top management team launched the ADWEA Strategic Transformation or ASTRO initiative. ASTRO aimed to build a Strategy Execution framework to align ADWEA with government's strategic goals and performance management framework and to improve operational performance and boost collaboration among companies in the sector.

What do you consider to be the most important Strategy Execution challenge for an executive team?

Between strategy development and Strategy Execution, the latter is often the toughest part. The key challenges that we see are:

- *Start with the right crew.* Without the right project team to drive the whole process, it's not going to work. And 'right' is not so much defined by skills as those can be developed or bought along the way – but by the synergy and chemistry between the team members. To avoid surprises, make sure that some have a good track record of working together. It goes without saying that each member needs to be a strong believer in the added value of Strategy Execution and convinced that the project is the right way forward for the organisation.

- *Get the top team onboard.* Without support from senior management, Strategy Execution becomes an uphill battle for the project team. So the first challenge is to secure the buy-in of senior management. How do you do this? By demonstrating some quick-win results and long-term benefits. Having the senior leaders onboard will facilitate the whole process and secure the right resources at the right time. The resource commitment is important. It's easy to say "Yes, we support the execution approach" but it's more difficult to realign the budget and provide the necessary resources to make it work. Their support is also crucial in ensuring that all units comply with the starting point, the corporate strategy. Transformational initiatives only work with commitment from the level above the silos. Without it, life for the execution team that's responsible for driving and monitoring these actions becomes very tough, if not impossible.

- ***Get middle management onboard.*** They play a key role in execution and you need their support. But they are busy doing their day-to-day work and don't want any new tasks added to their already heavy workload. So you need to cut through the 'workload' dilemma and get them on your side as they are often the crucial drivers of strategic initiatives. A good way to do this is by allocating the resources you secured from top management in an intelligent way.

- ***Get all employees onboard.*** Execution means everybody: people tend to think that Strategy Execution is the responsibility of the Strategy and Performance Department, but that's a mistake. It's the same as saying that quality is owned by the quality manager or people management by HR. So it's crucial to get everyone onboard. One crucial step to winning them over is to achieve a cultural shift, more specifically to create transparency. Strategy Execution needs close monitoring and people don't like to be monitored. The only way to avoid that conflict and gain their trust is to be very transparent. As long as they feel that Strategy Execution is like Big Brother watching them, they will not commit. So be transparent and take the time to communicate: explain why a solid Strategy Execution (including measuring) is important for the company and how this can also benefit their performance.

What Strategy Execution advice would you give to an ambitious manager?

- **Be ambitious, but realistic.** Your head can be above the clouds, but your feet need to stay on the ground. Aim high, but stay grounded. Manage expectations.
- **Have clear long-term goals, but also offer quick wins.** Concentrate on quick wins to demonstrate the benefits to senior manage-

ment. Strategy Execution is a long process and senior management wants fast results. In order to keep the commitment level high, make sure you offer the organisation quick wins.

- **Benchmark Strategy Execution.** Clearly identify the 'as is' situation before you start. Assess thoroughly the Strategy Execution starting position and conduct a similar exercise after each phase to demonstrate the achieved change. The data will help you secure commitment after the quick wins dry up. People also tend to forget very quickly. It helps if you have historical data to show clear progress and the added value of your execution project.

- **Recognise success.** When people do a great job, make sure you tell them. Offer them the recognition they deserve. It does not always have to be a pay rise.

Based on your experience, what are the classic Strategy Execution mistakes?

The two most common execution mistakes are:

1. **Too many KPIs**. Too many managers believe that the more you measure, the better your Strategy Execution. As a result, they introduce too many KPIs too early in the process. We have seen a company with 1200 KPIs. This way, you will probably lose more than you gain. The solution? Approach Strategy Execution in a different way, positioning and measuring it as one of the levers for success. Focus on the 10-20 measures that are crucial for tracking your strategy progress and keep operational measures where they belong – within the operational processes.

2. **The strategy director or department is not the strategy owner.** It's not because you have a privileged position in regard to the company strategy that you are the owner of the strategy, that you can enforce your view and your strategic ideas to the organisation. Strategy should be owned by the business units. The strategy department only facilitates the process of developing and monitoring the strategy. Accountability must be clear from the start.

Looking at Strategy Execution from a Balanced Scorecard perspective, what have been the most important benefits for your organisation?

The Balanced Scorecard has brought our leadership team a common way of understanding our strategic priorities and managing performance. Through the BSC, ADWEA and its group companies have developed a coordinated approach to strategic issues across areas such as people development and customer service. This new way of managing has enabled us to establish a performance-oriented culture and foster cultural change within our organisation.

It also brought us transparency in performance reporting, allowing management to monitor strategy success in a positive way. We established an end-to-end measurement system to monitor performance across the different distribution companies. There are over 200 people in the Balanced Scorecard community across the ADWEA Group who are actively involved in the development and reporting of the strategic objectives, KPIs and initiatives.

Last but not least, we now have a common approach to dealing with strategy and performance and all group companies speak the same language and share their issues.

PERFORMANCE TAKEAWAYS

- The Balanced Scorecard was invented by Art Schneiderman and made common knowledge by Kaplan and Norton.
- Today, the Scorecard is one of the most popular management instruments you will find in the execution arena.
- The Balanced Scorecard offers four specific benefits to an organisation:
    1. It breaks your strategy into smaller pieces.
    2. It measures strategy progress.
    3. It improves strategy communication, one of the weak spots of Strategy Execution.
    4. It develops the conceptual thinking power of individuals.
- Without a good connection to the overall strategy, the BSC just creates a bunch of measures that give you the feeling you are doing good when in fact you're not.
- The Balanced Scorecard is not the end goal, so don't stop the execution cascade.
- Analyse your current strengths and use 38 tips to your advantage.

And the answer is? 1000, 999, 998… take off (it can take some time)
The road a strategy has to travel along the path of the 8 is long and hard. It's easy to get lost. In large organisations, the strategy has to travel across five to eight layers before it reaches the bottom circle of the 8, the individual objectives.

So, the countdown to the strategy take-off, the moment between the design of the strategy PowerPoint and the real, individual action to turn this PowerPoint into action, can take some time. It's not a rocket launch where you get a big blast after 10 seconds. You need continuous effort for a longer period of time to get where you want to be. But if you stick to it, you will get there. Just make sure you don't drop the strategy stick on your way to the finish line!

PART 4

FEED THE 8

CHAPTER X

Challenge 8: Choose: pick a number between 1 and 10, said the magician

"Perception is strong and sight weak. In strategy it is important to see distant things as if they were close and to take a distanced view of close things"
– Miyamoto Musashi, legendary Japanese swordsman

"Strategy without tactics is the slowest route to victory. Tactics without strategy is the noise before defeat"
– Sun Tsu, ancient Chinese military general and strategist

"Strategy is thinking about a choice and choosing to stick with your thinking"

Strategy' is a cool word. Business people like to use it. It leaves a good impression with your audience if you talk about strategy. It's even expected from a certain seniority level in an organisation.

But 'strategy' is probably also the most over and misused word in business language. Most people who use it don't really know what strategy is all about. And I often have the impression that the more someone uses the word 'strategy' in a conversation, the less they know about the subject. It seems that strategy tourists in particular get a kick out of 'strategy talk'.

But why am I talking about strategy, you might ask yourself, as this is a book about Strategy Execution?

I have learnt over the years that proper knowledge about the fundamentals of strategy is crucial for a Strategy Execution Hero. Why?

First of all, *a solid Strategy Execution is driven by a solid strategy*. No matter how well you execute, if you set off in the wrong direction, all execution efforts are just a waste of time and energy. Think about the saying 'rubbish in, rubbish out'. An execution hero needs to know what a solid strategy is made of and should be able to spot a poor one and challenge it properly.

Secondly, if you have solid strategy skills you will be able to play a more *prominent role in the strategy building or update process*. Your colleagues will be eager to get you on board in the strategic thinking process. This in turn will give you an ideal starting position, an edge, to start executing as you will have a better understanding of the strategy (you helped develop it) and increased credibility (the one who helped design our future).

Finally, by knowing more about strategy, you will be able to *demystify the subject strategy* and uncover the strategy tourists with their fancy words that are void of content.

So it pays to invest in learning about strategy. In this chapter, I will uncover the basics of strategy, give you hints about how to find a strategic edge for your business, talk about Shared Value, a new trend in strategic thinking and, finally, provide ideas to spice up your strategy review process.

8 things every leader should know about strategy

Lots of research has been done on the topic and many books written. I have picked eight basics that I believe to be the best starting point.

Know these inside out and you will do better than 80 percent of the managers that you will come across. Want to dig deeper and reach 100 percent? Download the following reading list.

 Performance download 33. Great books on strategy – a reading list.

1. **The concept of strategy has been around for a long time**. The word 'strategy' originated from the world of ancient Greek military art. It is derived from the words 'stratos' meaning 'army' and 'agein' meaning 'to lead'. In its military aspect, the term derived from the stratagems by which a general sought to defeat an enemy, the plans he made for a campaign and the way he moved and disposed his forces in war.

2. **Compete to be unique, not to be the best.** Strategy is not about being the best, but about being unique. Competing to be the best in business is one of the major misconceptions about strategy. And if you only remember one tip from this list, it should be this one. Many leaders compare competition in business with the world of sports. There can only be one winner. But competing in business is more complex. There can be several winners. It does not have to be a zero sum game – you win, I lose or vice versa. Within a single industry, you can have several companies beating the industry average, each with a distinctive, different strategy. They are no direct threat to each other. There can be several winners. So the worst possible approach to strategy is to seek out the biggest player in the industry and try to copy everything they do.

3. **Compete for profit.** Business is not about having the largest market share or about growing fast. It's about making money. 'I want to grow my business' is not a strategy. 'I want to grow my business' is the same as saying, 'I want to be rich'. Those things (unfortunately) don't happen by themselves. Growing is not a strategy, it's a consequence.

When someone includes growth in their strategy, there should be an orange light starting to blink. That does not mean that you cannot use the word 'growth'. I use it a lot in the analysis phase – for example, when you talk about growth areas of the business or when you look for growth platforms – areas where you can reach potential that will give you additional profit.

4. **Know your industry**. A company is not an island – it's part of a larger ecosystem, an industry. Each industry has its own characteristics, its own structure. This structure and the relative position your company has within the industry determines profitability. Certain industries have a higher return than others. Your thinking about the industry and industry competition will determine your thinking about your strategy – how you are going to compete within the industry. The better you know and understand the industry, the better you will be able to determine elements that will make you stand out, be unique and reap a higher average return than the industry average.

5. **Choice**. In my eyes, this is the most simple strategy definition. You need a clear choice of *WHO* you are going to serve and a clear choice of *WHAT* you are going to serve those clients. It's about connecting the outside world – the demand side – with your company – the supply side. Or in fancy terms: you need a *value proposition* for a specific customer segment and unique activities in the *value chain* to serve them. The key word is 'choice'. You cannot be everything to everybody. You want to target a limited segment of potential buyers with the same needs. Next, you are going to tailor your activities in such a way that they meet these needs. Or in fancy terms: you want to tailor your value chain – your company's activities – to your value proposition. Strategic innovation is the process to make those choices – defining a new who and how for the organisation.

"Strategy is a pattern in a stream of decisions"
– Henry Mintzberg

---

6. **Learn to say no**. If you have clearly defined what you go for – a clear value proposition for a specific client segment (who) and a set of distinct, unique activities in your value chain to offer the needs of this client group (what), you will find out that there are lots of things that you are not going to do. There will be customers that you are not going to serve, activities that you are not going to perform and services/products that you will not be offering. In strategy, choosing what not to do is equally important. Using the words of the founding father of modern strategy thinking, Michael Porter: *"The essence of strategy is choosing what not to do"*. Each strategy should also have a section where it clearly states the noes. Ask yourself the following questions: "In our organisation, what do we say no to?", "Which customers in our industry do we make unhappy?" and, more practically, "Where did we systematically deliver a clear 'no' last year?". Be as specific as possible. A clear 'no' is a very good indication of a 'yes', a choice you or your company have made, maybe even without putting it in writing. So, when working on strategy, pay as much attention to the yeses as to the noes. In more academic terms: you need to know where your trade-offs are. You cannot be everything to everyone. If you decide to go north, you cannot go south at the same time.

7. **Don't ever stand still**. Having a good strategy means that you have arrived. Competitors move, customers' needs and behaviours change, technology evolves. One crucial element to determine a future path for your company is to predict these evolutions and trends and incorporate this thinking into the strategy-building process. If you don't, you can miss out on new value that is created in the industry or even left behind and get into trouble. Think about the smart phone and Nokia and you'll understand my point.

8. **Scenario thinking is important**. Facts and figures can only go so far. You need to turn data into assumptions that will fuel your reflection process. The standard way to work with assumptions in a structured way is by scenario thinking – fix some parameters and let other vary. This technique helps your reflection process by offering you possible future

routes (read: strategic options) for the company. I believe that scenario thinking is a crucial skill for anyone who wants to deal with strategy. Every leader should at least master the basics so that they don't need a strategy consultant for every reflection process or at least to help them challenge the scenario models that the strategy consultant presents.

Innovation + strategy = a dangerous cocktail in the hands of a strategy tourist

Like 'strategy', 'innovation' is a cool word. Put 'strategy' and 'innovation' in a single phrase and a strategy tourist starts to drool.

Like 'strategy', people use the word 'innovation' in a variety of ways. For some, it's all about technology and finding a technological edge, for others, it's about creativity. A third group will try to convince you that it's about attitude, culture and motivation and for the fourth group, it's about trying to predict future trends.

But the downside of all of these different definitions for the same word is that they become hollow and don't carry any meaning. It becomes very difficult for a leader to talk about the strategy of the organisation if everyone in the organisation defines the underlying words differently.

To be successful, I believe every leader has a double role. The first role is to be a strategy evangelist who takes on the challenge to cascade the company's strategy and preach about it at every occasion s/he gets. But to make this happen, a leader should also take on a second role, that of a strategy ambassador who promotes the concept and principles of strategy in general. When people understand the basic dynamics of strategy, they will much better understand the choices that are made and in particular why certain things are no longer done. I believe every leader has a crucial role in demystifying the concept of strategy in the company.

Where to find a strategic edge for your company

It's one thing to know what strategy is all about, but it's another to get out there and come up with one.

Let me start by saying that there is no magic formula for crafting the perfect strategy. If there was, the business world would look a lot different. But that does not mean there aren't a few shortcuts that you can take. What follows is a list with eight ingredients to inspire your strategic thinking, to find that edge that makes your company unique.

How does it work?

My favourite approach is to gather groups of people around the table and run a structured brainstorm around each of these topics. I've learnt that it works best when you keep the groups small (5-6 people) and the timing short (45 minutes). I tend to do four to six sessions. The output of the sessions is input for a more detailed analysis.

One important comment: in most organisations, this list will spark several good ideas. Before you put them in practice however, make sure you have a rough estimate of the future earnings for each idea. It's not enough to find value; the value potential has to be big enough to outweigh the effort (time and resources) capital that goes in. Think about it this way: if you have to feed three people, catching a chicken will help. But spending lots of time trying to catch the same animal when you have to feed a whole village is not smart. So make sure you look at the potential of the idea once you have found it. It you cannot roughly judge the future earnings, it often pays to do a test before launching yourself into a new adventure.

1. **Strengthen your current strategy**. The first thing you have to ask yourself is if it pays to strengthen your current position, to make your current strategy more distinctive (read: more unique). How? Look for ways to improve the current value proposition to your existing clients by further tailoring your value chain to their needs. Think about introducing new technology, features, products or services that leverage other areas in the value chain and fit with the current strategy. There are several benefits to strengthening what already exists rather than starting something new; you start from something that you know works today and that you can probably do quite quickly and is not disruptive. In short, you build on what you already have.

2. **Copy with pride**. Copying what others in your industry in your main markets are doing isn't smart as you will start competing on the same axes and that head-to-head competition will lead to price erosion. But copying can still pay off big time in these two cases:

   - **Inside your company:** This works very well for big companies but is often overlooked as it demands maturity to look across silos and admit that another division has done something great. The two key questions are: *"What activity in my divisional value chain can be copied or shared with other business units?"* and *"What can we copy from the others business units in our organisation?"*.

   - **Other geographical areas:** The world is a big place and many great companies only operate locally. But in this information era, it's easy to find them, learn from their success and see if some of their ingredients for success can be copied. As you are playing in different markets, there is no competition and therefore no risk of getting into a price war. *the performance factory* works with UNIZO, the federation for SMEs in Belgium and for 70 percent of the companies we looked at – about 80 companies – we found at least one great example in another geographical area that fuelled our strategic-thinking process.

3. **Go beyond the product**. Don't focus only on the product or service – a risk, especially in an engineering environment. There are more things to a value chain then the product itself. The key to a sustainable competitive advantage is that all activities are tailored to the value proposition.

4. **Recapture company heritage**. If your company has been around for some time, it follows that it has been doing something well for at least a certain time period. Finding out what that uniqueness is/was and reapplying it to boost your strategy is an interesting way of fuelling your reflection process about strategy. This doesn't mean that you have to re-do it in the same way, but an adapted version might be just what you need.

5. **Take advantage of a crisis.** Research shows that those companies

that leave the starting blocks first after a crisis often become industry leaders. Put differently, what you do during a crisis determines your strategic position once it's over. I will give lots of tips on this in the next section. In today's world, this is very interesting and provides some real opportunities if managed correctly.

6. **Build an execution edge.** Strategy Execution provides a competitive edge. A strategy needs to reinvent itself every five to seven years. Execution capabilities last much longer. So it pays off to invest in execution excellence.

7. **Learn to play with the business model.** A business model is a fancy word for the combination of choices you have made in your activities – your value chain – to bring your value proposition to life. The concept has been around for a long time, but for some reason, everyone apart from strategy consultants have forgotten about it. A recent book by Alexander Osterwalder in which he puts thinking about business models in an easy-to-use format has been a big hit. If you want to get going, identify activities and ask yourself some questions for each block. No inspiration? Have a look at the next exercise.

Exercise: Rethink your business model
Once you have identified the 'who' – your target customer segment(s), you need to organise the 'what' – your activities – in such a way that they offer unique value to your selected segment. To do this, you need to go through the different steps of your business model – think about sales, marketing, production, procurement, HR etc and make choices that create value for the client. To give you a feel for the kind of questions to ask, here's a list to get you started.
- Transactional versus recurring revenues
- Niche market versus mass market
- Capital expenditure versus partnership
- Product versus service
- Direct sales versus indirect sales

- Scale versus scope
- Personal versus automated
- Disruptive versus incremental
- Acquisition versus retention
- Human intensive versus system intensive
- One customer segment versus another
- Physical versus virtual
- Tailor-made versus mass production
- Fixed versus variable costs
- Paid versus free
- Distributed versus centralised
- In-sourcing versus out-sourcing
- Marketing versus sales
- New versus copy-paste

8. **Create social value.** Sustainability is a hot topic today and I believe it is more than a fad. Shared Value is a new concept that helps strategists to incorporate social value into the strategic positioning of an organisation. And it goes far beyond philanthropy. I will dig deeper into the topic in the following section of this chapter.

The next big thing in strategy thinking – Shared Value

Last year, I received an interesting phone call. The caller asked: *"Would you be interested in sharing your ideas about strategy and Strategy Execution with 600 senior executives at the Next Generation Strategy event?"*. After some reflection, I took on the challenge. The event was great. During Day 1, Roger Martin, Dean of the Rotman School of Management and Costas Markides, Professor of Strategic and International Management from the London Business School, talked about strategic thinking and strategic innovation. On Day 2, I shared the stage with Michael Porter, the godfather of strategy. One of the key topics Michael talked about was the concept of Shared Value. As I'm convinced that this will have a major impact on strategy thinking, I want to spend some time explaining the concept and my own views in the next section.

If you like to hear what I talked about during the Next Generation Strategy event, you can listen to a 60-minute recording or download the complete slide set.

 Performance download 34. The Next Generation Strategy Event – my slide set.

 Performance download 35. The Next Generation Strategy Event – 60 minute audio MP3.

The Shared Value concept explained

Let's start with Porter and Kremer's definition: *"You create shared value by enhancing the competitive position of a company while at the same time advancing the society in which it operates."*

The words 'at the same time' are very important. When people look at the relationship between a company and society, they tend to think it's a zero-sum game, a game with only one winner, like the concept of competition within an industry, as explained previously. When you do good for society, companies lose. When companies thrive, society doesn't benefit.

The strategy concept of Shared Value looks at the positive sum. It means that certain choices will strengthen the strategic position of the organisation, certain activities in the value chain and at the same time offer benefits for society. In fact, it is looking for those elements in your value chain – your company's activities – that gives you an edge and helps you advance at the same time. An example: Nestlé needs high-quality raw materials to produce first-class dairy products. When they entered the market in India in the Moga district in 1962, local farmers were not able to consistently deliver this quality. Only 180 farmers passed the test. Nestlé worked with local farmers to improve their production techniques and long-term contracts to buy products at a fair price. Today there are 75,000 farmers that reach Nestlé's quality standards. In the Moga region, they have five times more doctors than other regions of India, better primary schools and basic needs such as electricity are fulfilled.

3 generations of Corporate Social Responsibility: Donators, Avoiders and Creators

Reducing the effects of CO2, fighting poverty and cradle-to-cradle: topics that you will find on quite a few corporate agendas today. But are they launched with a positive sum effect in mind or are there other motives in play?

I'm not sure. I think it depends on the company. When I look around, I see three Corporate Social Responsibility generations that I call the *Donators*, *Avoiders* and *Creators*. Let's take a closer look.

The first CSR generation is made up of Donators. They are good citizens who believe in the traditional trade-off between organisations and society, but want to give something back to society, to compensate. The good cause is often randomly selected and driven by the personal preferences of a few individuals, most often the owner or CEO. There is no ambition to strengthen the strategic positioning, but many use it to look good to the outside world and as an advertising campaign on their annual report or website.

In fact, I believe that quite a few Donators engage in CSR to create goodwill and keep off the activists' radar. Let me explain. The world around us is changing. The general public has taken a new position – sustainability has become the new norm, at least from a lip service perspective. Saying you are against sustainability is simply not done in today's world. In Europe you'd be signing your death warrant. In this new world, activists are also more aggressive and look for 'bad' examples that they can use and abuse in their campaigns. So what do Donators do? They try to create (read: buy) goodwill through CSR. They commit an amount of money to show the world that they are sustainable; they give their annual report a nice green shine, put some trees or windmills on the front page and show nice pictures of smiling people with their executive in some far-off country. And the costs are written off as an expense. CSR is a smart move, like point of sale material or a marketing campaign that wins the hearts of consumers.

> *"Corporate Social Responsibility should be about more than colouring your annual report green and giving a bag of money to your favorite charity in return for some nice pictures"*

The second CSR generation is made up of the Avoiders. Their main objective is to reduce any negative impact of their own activities. Avoiders are aware that certain activities from their value chain have a negative impact on society and they try to reduce the negative impact. A good example is those organisations that are trying to reduce their energy use.

The third CSR generation are the Creators. This group embraces the Shared Value concept and view sustainability as a positive sum game. They see Corporate Social Responsibility as an investment, not an expense. They are also much more selective about the activities they target. They believe that no business can solve all of society's problems so a worthy cause is not good enough. They focus on those social issues that affect the drivers of a company's competitiveness in the locations in which it operates.

Where is your company at and where do you want to be? The answer isn't black and white as most companies don't fit clearly into one generation. But if I were to ask you to take the 80/20, you will most probably be able to pin it down.

Sustainability is more than the latest hype. Sustainability will become a strategic differentiator and those companies that find ways to create shared value will have a better competitive position. This does not mean that you have to jump on the bandwagon without pausing for thought. Each company is unique with its own specific value chain, choice of strategy and geographical presence. Not every country looks at sustainability in the same way or has the same growth challenges, but these should not be excuses to ignore the topic in your reflection process about your company's strategy, a scenario where the company focuses on creating shared value.

Shared Value is a topic that is getting more and more attention. It has become one of my more popular keynotes over the last year. Want to know more? You can download my slide set. It could be a good starting point to fuel your thinking and launch a debate about CSR in your team, division or company.

 Performance download 36. *3 generations CSR: Donators, Avoiders and Creators* – my slide set.

Spice up your strategy process (in times of crisis)

What separates great companies from good ones? Bestselling author Jim Collins tackles the interesting problem of 'How to do better when you are doing well' in his bestseller *From Good to Great.* But what do you do if things are not going well and you are faced with a crisis – a situation many organisations, at least for part of their business, face in an economic downturn?

Over the last two years, I have worked with many organisations that were good or even great but were seriously hit by the crisis. In this section, I want to highlight and share some of their learnings in the field. More specifically, I would like to zoom in on how they went back to the strategy drawing board and prepared for recovery. I would like to offer you a recipe to spice up your strategy process in tough times.

There are three sections. All three will help you prepare for strategy recovery, each one tackling recovery from a different perspective. This first section looks more closely at the strategy review itself. The second section covers the budget cycle and the third addresses the people challenges.

As before, you can download a checklist and spend some time analysing these dynamics before you start your strategy exercise. Alternatively, you might want to put these dynamics on the table during the first step of your strategy review process and use them to animate a lunch or dinner discussion. Whatever approach you choose, I'm convinced that a sound reflection process, whether alone or in a group, will bring creativity to your strategy review discussions and realism to its execution: two crucial elements for success.

 Performance download 37. Spice up your strategy process – a checklist.

 Performance download 38. Spice up your strategy process – workshop format.

But before you dive into the tips, let me answer the important question "When do you need to start with the recovery?".

Let's be honest. Not everyone will survive every crisis. But most will. And the future success of these companies will be influenced by the decisions and actions taken during the crisis. Those who haven't prepared may survive the recession only to find themselves overtaken by their competitors as the economy gets back to normal. Take a look at these figures from an article in the *Harvard Management Update* (Baveja, Ellis, Rigby, March 2008). A recent study of more than 700 companies over a six-year period found that *"Twice as many companies made the leap from laggards to leaders during the last recession (90-91) as during surrounding periods of economic calm"*. And most of these changes lasted long after the recession was over – a clear indication that what you do during the crisis determines your position when it's over. Or, just surviving the crisis isn't enough. So the point is that you need to start to prepare for recovery *during* a crisis. In other words, you need to start the strategy review process earlier than your instinct tells you to. Let's now look at how you can do that.

Go beyond the classical Porter analysis

When a crisis hits, corporations start downsizing – from trimming the fat to crash diets. And as a result, the long-term focus gets buried under short-term priorities. But how do you get going again when there's light at the end of the tunnel, when those forgotten strategic topics once again pop up on the radar screen.

The first thing you will probably notice when you submerge is that it's not business as usual anymore as the industry you operate in has changed dramatically.

Therefore, your strategy review – the kick-start of every strategy process – needs an extra punch. You want – and probably need – that extra something that helps you and your company digest the changed environment and prepare for a strong recovery. I believe that the classical elements of a sound strategy review is the basis... but that's not enough. You need to dig deeper into existing analysis areas and be creative by looking at others. Here's a list of eight dynamics you should integrate into your upcoming strategy review process. Some build on classical strategy analysis and will hold no surprises for you. Others are probably new analysis areas and challenge you to look beyond the obvious.

1. Economic dynamics

This is the obvious one. The one you hear on the news every day. The one you most probably know best and have integrated already. This is all about macro indicators telling us what happened in the past, while economists (try to) predict what is going to happen and politicians try to stabilise the market. These dynamics should definitely be included, but only in your basis as you start. Don't limit yourself to listening to what others write or say, but dig in. What does it really mean? How acute is the danger? What does it mean for my sector, for my company?

2. People dynamics

It's impossible to win without the right people. So ask yourself the following questions: Who's still in your company? Are they going to stay or are they just waiting for the right moment to leave? As you know, the job market follows a pattern different from that of the economy so when do you expect the job market to pick up again?

3. Budget dynamics

How fast can we make budget changes? An interesting question when you know that the last budget was made in the midst of one of the largest economic crises of all time. Yours and your colleagues' current budget ideas are most probably coloured strongly by the current crisis and are very cost-driven. But watch out for the boomerang! If the financial climate improves, you might be stuck with an inflexible budget. So look at the budget dynamics in your company and evaluate the time needed to shift gears when necessary. You'll find more tips on this in the next section.

4. Industry dynamics

Some of your competitors won't survive the crisis. Others will, but they will definitely look different. They might have had an extreme make-over. And there will be new players in the market – competitors, suppliers, and customers too. In other words, business won't be as usual. You'll need to find out how the crisis has affected – and will continue to affect – the dynamics in your industry with all the different players involved – from customers and private and public investors to suppliers and partners and to existing and new competitors. KPMG research involving 852 companies in 29 countries indicates that about 50 percent of the companies are changing – or planning to change – their business model (reported in *De Tijd*, 3 June 2009). Find out why changes have occurred in your industry, predict what is going to change and see how all of this can be played to your advantage.

If you haven't done an industry analysis or you want to review the work that you have done, take a look at download 39. It explains the basic steps of an industry analysis.

 Performance download 39. Typical steps in an industry analysis – overview.

5. Customer dynamics

You were well aware of your customers' needs before the crisis. But do you know what they are today? The chances are that the difficult economic climate has altered your customers' 'needs' or loyalties dramatically. So don't rely on past research — do your homework. You might be very surprised by the results.

6. Decision dynamics

The crisis has scared many executives. They have become hyper-vigilant and avoid taking risks. Long-term decisions are postponed until things stabilise. Be bold and put this on the table. I'm not saying that you need to take risks. You might want to be more careful about certain decisions than you were before, but you don't want to become paralysed either. Each executive team should put this at the top of the agenda.

7. Execution dynamics

Take into account what you can do. Restructuring has a negative impact on morale and impacts your change capacity as well. Good people have left or are leaving. Your remaining managers' stress levels are very high. Proper supporting processes might be at risk. The key takeaway is: a previously approved strategy could very well be less realistic today due to reduced execution capacity in your organisation. It's crucial to take this into account now!

8. Leadership dynamics

Last but not least, you should look carefully at the captains on your ship. How well did they perform during this extreme crisis situation? Any signs of burn-out? Is their style suitable to guiding the company through the recovery period?

Avoid the budget boomerang

In many organisations, budget is king. It's like the Amazon, the source of life. The strategy process is more like a small stream that meanders slowly through the organisation (and if you're unlucky, the water doesn't flow at all and starts to smell).

So what does this mean? If your budget is not in line with your new recovery strategy, it's not going to work. Your budget needs to reflect your strategy. If you don't find the important elements of your recovery plan in the company budget, it does not exist.

But changing budgets in large organisations is like changing the course of an oil tanker. It's very slow. Moreover, the alignment process between strategy and budget is not managed actively, resulting in more delays and frustration with those who came up with the new recovery course.

Want to avoid all this?

Here are seven tips to help you get it done.

Tip 1: Start with a solid strategy review. Don't rush into the budget exercise. This year, budgeting isn't business as usual. Even when your company isn't directly impacted by the crisis, the competitive landscape in which it operates will be. So spend the extra time reviewing your strategy and make sure that you map the different dynamics that impact on your company.

Tip 2: Don't stop restructuring. Finish what you started. Don't stop the restructuring mid-point. That would be the worst thing to do. Remember, successful Strategy Execution also means successfully executing your restructuring initiatives. So make sure you finish the restructuring you have planned. Don't leave any loose ends – plan the financial and human resources in your budget to tie them up.

Tip 3: Think like Johan Cruijff. One of the most successful trainers and players of all time is known for the words: *"Every advantage has its disadvantage and vice versa"*. You just need to look for them. An example: the current economic climate creates cost consciousness. Use this to your advantage. Take a cost conscious approach to your budgeting. Areas where it would have been impossible to discuss cost reductions might be put on the table today – especially if you base your competitive advantage on the cost side, ride out the wave completely and take advantage of the cost awareness business climate. Keep everyone on a tight budget leash.

Tip 4: Debate assumptions. Now even more than ever. Discuss the 'why' behind each budget line. Don't let people seduce you with the line, *"But that's always been budgeted for"*.

Tip 5: Don't put the support departments on a yo-yo, stop-go diet. They are often caught by surprise and respond reactively resulting in a short-term, stop-go strategy. As a result, the department ends up worse off than before. Support departments need a long-term vision as well as a budget approach. Make sure you know the end game – the business model that you would like to aim for – and look ahead at flexible budget solutions as preparation to shift when the time is right.

Tip 6: Review all project spending. Don't just relaunch a project that has been put on hold. Before you know it, you are back at business as usual with the old, revived projects sucking up all available resources (and therefore money). Don't assume that what was needed before the crisis is needed today. Re-evaluate, challenge and budget accordingly.

Tip 7: Make sure you are ready for the turnaround. The crisis will end. It won't happen overnight, but it is just a question of time. Most companies however will be defining their budgets taking only the current situation into account. And budgets are like oil tankers – they need time to change course. So discuss today how the company can react swiftly when opportunities do arise. You don't want to be left standing on the deck of your oil tanker, watching all the opportunities pass you by unable to stop and turn to chase after them.

Build an execution edge

Without the right execution skills, you won't succeed. You know this by now. I'm sure you knew this even before you started reading this book. But as you also know, there is a difference between knowing and doing.

I'm a strong believer in integrating execution thinking into the strategy exercise. And especially when the going gets tough, you will need to pay special attention to specific elements of your execution capabilities. Here's my list:

Tip 1: Evaluate your execution capabilities. Your execution capabilities will help your organisation deliver the strategy and turn it into performance. However, in times of crisis, organisations often accidentally cut out some of the skills, processes, technologies, values and assets that make up these core competencies, causing an entire competency to weaken or even disappear. Think about the cuts that were made during the crisis and evaluate the damage done to the overall execution strengths.

Tip 2: Prepare to hire great people. The labour market hibernates when the economy slows down. If you stopped investing in employer branding, the moment you start discussing recovery is the time to get going again. Also, make an inventory today of the people you will need and develop ideas for how to get them. You want to be in the front row when people feel secure enough to start looking for a new job.

Tip 3: Develop your employees. Most organisations have cut their development budget drastically. And while this was often done out of necessity, it's a situation that cannot last forever. It doesn't mean going back to the usual training plan. In fact, it's smart to rethink and improve the development approach in your organisation. It may be a good moment to review your development approach and see how you can do more with less. Most companies I know can reduce their development spending by 20 to 25 percent while simultaneously increasing quality by 10 to 15 percent. It just requires the right burning platform. And that's not an issue in today's business environment.

Tip 4: Decide today how you will monitor execution tomorrow. You don't want to hear from the accounting department six months down the line as to whether your execution programme is on track or not. You need real-time and leading (read: predicting) indicators that will give you early warning signs as to if and how you need to change course. And as each execution is unique, there is no fixed set of indicators that will work in every situation. So it's important that you get into the habit of building and monitoring your own dashboard that is adapted to the needs of the specific execution challenge. So start building that dashboard today.

Tip 5: Find time. How to carve out enough time to create capacity is a crucial question that needs an answer. Finding the time to do certain tasks seems to be the key challenge of the current times. Everyone is too busy. Everyone is running on their treadmills as fast as they can. But if people don't have time available, they won't be able to execute a strategy. So creating capacity to get things done is a major challenge and often requires not only prioritisation skills, but also solid negotiation and influencing skills to get things moving.

Tip 6: Manage stress. For most individuals, a crisis is a stressful period in their business life. And quite a few of them are stretched to the limit, with burn-out risks just around the corner. When the economy picks up, your company will need to shift gears again, demanding that people go the extra mile. There is a risk that this could prove a push too far. Be aware of the impact that the crisis has had and continues to have on the energy levels of people in your organisation and take action to restore the balance before jumping into a new adventure.

PERFORMANCE TAKEAWAYS

- The chapter starts with eight things that every leader should know about strategy. Some of the key points are: strategy is all about choice, about being unique rather than about being the best, there can be several winners in an industry – it's not a zero-sum game where someone always loses if you win.
- 'Strategy' is a fancy word. Managers use it because it sounds cool. But without the right meanings, the word becomes hollow. You can be different by demystifying strategy and teaching people the right meanings.
- There is no magic formula to find a strategic edge for your company, but there are a few ingredients that can get you on the right track. Use the eight levers described in this chapter to find unique value for your company.
- 'Shared Value' is a new concept in strategy thinking. Include the ideas into your strategy reflection process and see how they can make your company even more unique.
- There are three generations of Corporate Social Responsibility: Donators, Avoiders and Creators. Where does your company fit in? And where would you like it to be?
- When you are faced with a crisis, your strategy process needs an extra boost to prepare for recovery. Use the tips in this chapter to your advantage.

And the answer is? Pick any number between 1 and 10, said the magician
For me, strategy in the simplest form is *"thinking about a choice and choosing to stick with your thinking"*. And although the future is hard to predict, the choice you make is not random. It's based on the best knowledge you have today about a variety of parameters that you turned into assumptions to help you make a deliberate decision. When you do a trick with a magician, it seems random, but it's not. It looks like magic, but it is a combination of a thorough understanding of the underlying factors that make a trick work or not and a lot of practice to get it right.

BIBLIOGRAPHY

Borg, James. *Persuasion*. Pearson Education Limited.

Bossidy, Larry and Charan, Ram. *Execution*. Random House Business Books.

Branche, Alan P. and Bodley-Scott, Sam. *Implementation*, McGraw Hill.

Brinkerhoff, Robert O. *The Success Case Method*. Berrett-Koehler Publishers Inc.

Buttrick, Robert. *The Project Workout: The Ultimate Handbook of Project and Programme Management*. Prentice Hall.

Davidson Frame, J. *Project Management Competence*. Jossey-Bass.

Davis, Scott M and Dunn, Michael. *Building the Brand-driven Business*. Jossey-Bass.

De Wit, Bob and Meyer, Ron. *Strategy: Process, Content, Context*. South-Western College Pub.

Dewilde, Dennis and Anderson Geoff. *The Performance Connection*. Walkerville Publishing Inc.

Dixit, Avinash and Nalebuff, Barry. *The Art of Strategy*. W.W.Norton & Co.

Englund, Randall L. Graham, Robert J. and Dinsmore, Paul C. *Creating the Project Office*. Jossey-Bass.

Flannery, Thomas P., Hofrichter, David A. and Platten Paul E. *People, Performance & Pay*. The Free Press – a division of Simon & Schuster Inc.

Graham, Robert J. and Englund, Randall L. *Creating an Environment for Successful Projects*. Jossey-Bass.

Gratton, Lynda. *Living Strategy*. Pearson Education Limited.

Hall, Brian J. *Performance Management*. Harvard Business Essentials. Harvard Business School Press.

Hawkins, Peter and Smith, Nick. *Coaching, Mentoring and Organizational Consultancy*. Open University Press, McGraw-Hill Education.

Hindle, Tim. *Guide to Management Ideas*. *The Economist* in association with Profile Books Ltd.

Hrebiniak, Lawrence G. *Making Strategy Work*. Wharton School Publishing.

Jeffreys, Michael. *Success Secrets of the Motivational Superstars*. Prima Publishing.

Jones, Phil. *Communicating Strategy*. Gower Publishing Limited.

BIBLIOGRAPHY

Kaplan, Robert S. and Norton, David P. *The Execution Premium*. Harvard Business Press.

Kim, W. Chan, Mauborgne, Renée. *Blue Ocean Strategy*. Harvard Business School Press.

Magretta, Joan. *Understanding Michael Porter.* Harvard Business Review Press

Maslen, Andy. *Write to Sell*. Marshall Cavendish Limited and Cyan Communications Limited.

Massmore, Jonathan. *Excellence in Coaching*. Kogan Page Limited.

Michaelson, Gerald A. *Sun Tzu: The Art of War for Managers*. Adams Media.

Morgan, Mark, Levitt, Raymond E. and Malek William. *Executing your Strategy*. Harvard Business School Press.

Nutt, Paul C. *Why decisions fail*. Berrett-Koehler Publishers, Inc.

Porter, Michael. *Competitive Strategy*. Free Press.

Porter, Michael E. *Competitive Strategy: Techniques for Analyzing Industries and Competitors*. Free Press.

Schwartz, David J. *The Magic of Thinking Big*. Simon & Schuster UK Ltd.

Senge, Peter M. *The Fifth Discipline*. Doubleday – a division of Bantam Doubleday Dell Publishing Group, Inc.

Speculand, Robin. *Bricks to Bridges*. Bridges Business Consultancy Int.

Stern, Carl W. and Stalk George jr. *Perspectives on Strategy*. John Wiley & Sons, Inc.

Stettinius, Wallance, Wood jr, Robley D., Doyle Jacqueline L. and Colley jr, John L. *How to Plan and Execute a Strategy*. Mighty Manager series. McGraw Hill.

Stiffler, Mark A. *Performance*. John Wiley & Sons, Inc.

Vitale, Joe. *Hypnotic Writing*. John Wiley & Sons, Inc.

Waal de, André A. *Power of Performance Management*. John Wiley & Sons, Inc.

Weiss, Tracey B. Hartle, Franklin. *Performance Management*. St. Lucie Press.

Whitmore, John. *Coaching for Performance*. Nicholas Brealey Publishing.

Wilson, Carol. *Best Practice in Performance Coaching*. Kogan Page Limited.

INDEX

Symbols

8, The 23
  building blocks 23
  Cascade 24
  Communicate 24
  Compare and learn 25
  Evaluate performance 27
  extended 28
  framework 21
  Manage initiatives 26
  Monitor and coach 27
  Review and update your strategy 23
  Set objectives 26
80/20 6
95 percent rule 152

A

action learning 179
ADWEA 8, 218, 219, 222
Alexander, Graham 94
alignment 19
  horizontal 19
Allaf, Tufic 218
Al Nuaimi, Abdullah 218
Arthur D. Little 71
audience 68, 70, 71, 74, 76, 81, 106, 140
AXA IX

B

Balanced Scorecard 14, 21, 25, 57, 62, 89, 125, 127, 136, 181
Bannister, Roger 41, 42
Barometer® 9, 15, 78, 262
Base IX
Batman 1
benchmark 15, 30, 53, 58, 135, 144, 262
best-in-class 9, 20, 21, 44, 50, 73, 133, 136, 148, 170, 186, 189
Blaise, Pascal 63

INDEX

INDEX

eBay 2, 8, 162
Einstein, Albert 121
e-learning 81, 180
elephant 145, 165
experts 2, 82, 261

F

Facilitation Rainbow 71
FAQ (Frequently Asked Questions) 138
FedEx 114, 186
feedback 9, 15, 23, 27, 44, 49, 51, 76, 84, 87, 97, 103, 108, 135, 141, 142,
    143, 156
Feyfer, Frederick 261
Fifth Discipline, The 48
Forbes 42

G

Gallwey, Tim 96
gap 2, 14, 30, 159, 176
Gates, Bill 61
GDFSuez IX
Glasgow, Arnold H. 41
goal-setting 42, 43, 45, 50, 51, 58
Goleman, Daniel 169
Guevara, Carlos XI, 197

H

Half, Robert 166
Harvard Business Review (HBR) 2, 13, 92
Hawkins, Peter 109, 251
Hepburn, Katharine 91
Hoffmann, Hans 121
Holme, Thomas Timings 20
Honda IX
Hoskins, Siân 261
Hrebiniak 21, 251
Hulk, The Incredible 1

INDEX

INDEX

Malek 147
Martin, Chuck 8, 61, 139
matrix 25, 129, 134, 135, 149
Maxwell, Alan 8, 139
McClelland, David 169
McKinsey 146
measurement 19, 20, 135, 183, 184
Merck 18
Microsoft 61
Minto, Barbara 63, 64
Morgan 147
Motorola 176

N

Norton 2, 14, 21, 29, 30, 151, 194, 196, 208, 223, 252
Norton, David 193
Novo Nordisk 8, 82
Nutt, Paul 160, 252

O

objective setting: see goal setting 16, 26, 42, 44, 47, 50, 52, 58, 62, 79, 84, 86, 89, 100, 125, 171

P

Palladium 146
performance 63
  -driven 1, 140, 161
  management 144
  story 9, 136, 137, 138, 144
performance coach 101
Performance coaching 27, 92, 93, 95
Performance takeaways 30, 37, 58, 89, 116, 144, 165, 189
Performance tip 25, 46, 66, 69, 77, 79, 96, 131, 134, 135, 160, 179
Philadelphia Story, The 91
PMI 155
Porras 18
Porter, Michael E 231, 236, 237, 242, 252

INDEX

INDEX

NOTES

ACKNOWLEDGEMENTS

I want to thank everyone involved in the creation of this book, many of whom I'll forget to mention by name, so forgive me.

First of all, the experts and senior executives who contributed to this book; for their wisdom and support in helping me shape my thoughts.

The research team – Els, Tom, Anne, Maaike, Marieke and Pauwelijn – for the long hours and respecting of deadlines and everyone else from *the performance factory* for their commitment to this project.

Thanks also to my editor Siân Hoskins – a true word wizard – and Fré Feyfer, the art master, from Uncompressed.

To the clients who are constantly aiming at improving performance and especially Erik Dralans who was kind enough to allow me to quote the intranet example from ING.

And last but not least, a huge thanks to my wife Karen and kids Lauren and Jonas for supporting me all the way through this book project.

Thank you all.